D0772627

Over There

NUMBER ONE:
C. A. Brannen Series

Over There

A Marine in the Great War

by Carl Andrew Brannen

Preface and Annotation by
Rolfe L. Hillman, Jr.,
and
Peter F. Owen

Afterword by
J. P. Brannen

TEXAS A&M UNIVERSITY PRESS
College Station

The paper used in this book meets the minimum requirements
of the American National Standard for Permanence
of Paper for Printed Library Materials, Z39.48-1984.
Binding materials have been chosen for durability.
∞

Unless otherwise noted, photographs were supplied
by the Brannen family, and maps were drafted by Cartographics
at Texas A&M University.

Library of Congress Cataloging-in-Publication Data

Brannen, Carl Andrew, b. 1899.
    Over there : a marine in the Great War / by Carl
Andrew Brannen ; preface and annotation by Rolfe L.
Hillman, Jr. and Peter F. Owen ; afterword by J.P. Brannen.
        p.   cm. — (C.A. Brannen series no. 1)
    Includes bibliographical references and index.
    ISBN 0-89096-690-7 (cloth : alk. paper)
    1. Brannen, Carl Andrew, b. 1899. 2. World War,
1914–1918—Campaigns—France. 3. World War, 1914–
1918—Personal narratives, American. 4. United States.
Marine Corps. Marine Brigade, 4th. Regiment, 6th.
Company, 80th—History. 5. United States. Marine
Corps—Biography. 6. Marines—United States—Biography.
I. Hillman, Rolfe L. II. Owen, Peter F. III. Series.
D548.B73   1996
940.4'144—dc20   95-43731
                                                      CIP

Contents

Illustrations

C. A. BRANNEN'S SCRAPBOOK

Beginning page 71

J. P. BRANNEN'S SCRAPBOOK
Beginning page 109

Bulldog fountain at Belleau
C. A. Brannen's dog tags
Lion Fountain at Bouresches
Chauchat and Hotchkiss at Marine Corps Museum
Sunken road where Brannen was pinned
Ruins of sugar beet mill at Villemontoire
Undeveloped road taken by Major Williams
Clearing at Kilduff ambush site
Location of Germans
Capt. David R. Kilduff's marker
Hindenberg line bunker
View from Essen trench toward Hill 210
Road atop Blanc Mont
German dugout
Street scene of Les Isolettes
Meuse where attempts to place footbridges failed
Site Where Brannen Crossed Rhine
German soldier memorial
Carl A. Brannen, Jr. at Texas A&M University
C. A. Brannen during World War II

MAPS

It may occur to the reader that the central and critical incident in this small book containing a soldier's memoirs occurred on October 3, 1918, when, during the 6th Marines' attack on Blanc Mont Ridge, a German bullet broke C. A. Brannen's bayonet off at the stub. When the action subsided, one of his company mates observed, "Old Brannen stuck his bayonet in one and broke it off!"

Although Brannen didn't realize it at the time or identify it later, this moment must have been for him an epiphany—a simple and striking event that allows us, these many years later, to grasp how he saw combat and how he came to see himself.

On these pages we encounter a man nineteen years old, one who marches a long and severely difficult path after, in January, 1918, in the middle of his second year at Texas A&M College, he goes to war. He experiences Marine Corps training, the movement to France, and the stark experience of mortal combat, first as a new replacement and then as an experienced member of a team. While his company mates disappear as casualties at Belleau Wood, St. Mihiel, and Soissons, he is concerned with the men immediately around him; he thrives on admiration of, and identification with, his platoon leader, his company commander. His memoirs show little or no identification with, or concern for the actions of, those men of higher rank who, at some remote location, plan tactics and make command decisions—and thereby dictate his fate. By October 3, he has established his group identification and obviously has earned the approbation of his peers. His friends by now assume that Brannen will know exactly how to handle his bayonet at close quarters. Brannen did not find it necessary to correct their opinion.

Such are the fundamental factors, the individual and group loyalties, that motivate men to acquit themselves well in combat. Brannen, wounded in battle and in the hospital system for three weeks, goes on with 80th Company through the Meuse-Argonne campaign to the armistice on November 11; pulls his months of duty in the occupation of the Rhineland; and, at its end, earns a place in the Composite Regiment of men picked to represent the American Expeditionary Forces in the many ceremonial events of 1919.

Brannen set down these memoirs sometime in the late 1930s, almost twenty years later. Without doubt, he must have spent many sad hours reflecting on the loss of his close comrades. Nevertheless, it seems to me, as a late-coming reader selected to comment on the memoirs, that Brannen's predominant feeling about his Marine Corps service was not morose sadness but great pride. He had done it all, he had done it well, and he never got a rating higher, in his view, than a comrade's admiring though mistaken remark: "Old Brannen stuck his bayonet in one and broke it off!"

In 1988, Dr. Samuel Hynes taught a Princeton University course on war literature. He concentrated on the memoirs of ordinary soldiers from the Napoleonic Wars to Vietnam, excluding novels and the memoirs of generals. "It is a literature not much studied, or even read, except by military historians and war buffs," he said. "And yet, when you think about it, war is one subject that has been continuous in the human story."

Hynes observed that memoirs serve the two different requirements of reporting and remembering. C. A. Brannen, who left no "reporting" in the form of a diary or letters from France, clearly set down these pages as a form of remembering; even that task was undertaken at the insistence of his wife. Brannen had not a photographic memory; indeed, his account would have been more coherent and comprehensive had it been subjected to the methodology of a modern historian doing an oral history interview. But that didn't happen; what we have, often in striking understatement, is a set of fragments that Hynes calls "the remembered war that persists in the mind through a lifetime."

It must be kept in mind that I have not edited what Brannen wrote. Only minor changes have been made in the typescript given me by Brannen's daughter, Frances Brannen Vick, Dallas, Texas. I have, rather, given explanatory and sometimes critical notes and comments. These appear in introductory sections at the beginning of each chapter and in endnotes. By this function, I have acquired the title "Annotator."

—Rolfe L. Hillman
Arlington, Virginia

Midway through his annotation, Colonel Hillman suffered a medical setback which forced him to seek assistance to finish this book. I feel fortunate and flattered that Colonel Hillman invited me to assist him. As a patient mentor, the colonel taught me how to carry research into published writing. As a lifelong soldier, he lived a daily example of the values of "duty-honor-country." Tragically, he passed on before publication was completed.

Rolfe Hillman and Carl Brannen were cut from the same cloth. As young men, they served their country without hesitation. In combat they fought in some of the most difficult actions in our nation's history. Having survived, they put pen to paper, in the hope they could pass on something of their experience to the next generation.

We have prefaced each chapter with enough detail for the casual reader to place Brannen's experience in historical context. The notes provide amplifying detail for the serious researcher. We have left the text to stand alone. The depth of Carl Brannen's experience is evident form his words.

—Peter F. Owen

Acknowledgments

The annotators wish to acknowledge the generous
assistance of the following institutions and individuals: Brig. Gen. Edwin H. Simmons, USMC (Ret.),
Marine Corps Historical Center, Washington, D.C.
Navy Yard, and his staff, especially Danny J.
Crawford; J. Michael Miller and the staff of the
Marine Corps Research Center, Quantico, Virginia;
The Still Photo Collection, National Archives, Washington, D.C., which provided many of the photographs; the Congressional Medal of Honor Society,
Patriot's Point, South Carolina; Otranto Branch,
Charleston County Public Library, North Charleston, South Carolina; William McQuade at the Nimitz
Library, U.S. Naval Academy, Annapolis, Maryland,
who helped track down information about USS
Henderson and the naval railway batteries; George
Clark, Pike, New Hampshire, who unselfishly provided numerous details from his extensive private library of Marine Corps history; George MacGillivray,
Jr., Arlington, Virginia, a Second World War marine, who provided photographs and insight from
his father's service with the 80th Company in France;
William W. Sellers, Lexington, Missouri, who per-

mitted us to cite from his father's memoir of service with the 78th Company; and Col. John E. Greenwood, USMC (Ret.), and his staff at the Marine Corps Association, Quantico, Virginia. We are especially grateful for the patient support of our families.

The Brannen family wishes to acknowledge that the photographs included in the first photo section were taken by C. A. Brannen as a soldier during World War I.

During World War I, a brigade of American marines fought on land in France. Of 8,000 men in this group, more than half, or 5,073 men and 126 officers, became casualties. This book is a brief account of these troops by one of the survivors, Carl Andrew Brannen. The experiences recited were acquired during participation on the following battle fronts in 1918: Belleau Woods of the Château-Thierry sector, Soissons, Pont-a-Mousson, St. Mihiel, Blanc Mont Ridge, and the Meuse-Argonne battle.

No attempt is made to record the larger aspects of that particular war; I only present a few incidents [from the point of view] of a soldier in the ranks. In addition to the phases of the battles of this brigade, recordings are made of the training camp, the Army of Occupation, and my experiences as a member of the Composite Regiment or General Pershing's Honor Guard.

The time involved is approximately twenty-one months, divided as follows: Parris Island, South Carolina, three months; Quantico, Virginia, one month; France, nine months; Germany, six months; Belgium, Luxembourg, and England combined, one month.

In addition, two weeks were spent in New York and the Marine Barracks in Washington, D.C.

Of the many acts of heroism by a body such as this, very few ever get into print. Many times during the defense of a position, the entire Marine force was massacred. At other times an attacking contingent was obliterated, leaving few if any survivors. This book is dedicated to the dead and the living of this Marine brigade, which earned from the Germans the sobriquet "Devil Dogs." This task is undertaken that the descendants of those who made the heroic sacrifices in the 4th Marine Brigade may have some of the memories preserved to them.

The well-scarred but profusely decorated banners of the 5th and 6th Regiments of the 4th Marine Brigade have been carried into battle since 1918, but no American now or in the future will ever have to make excuses for the actions of the 4th Marine Brigade in 1918.

—Carl Andrew Brannen

Over There

Parris Island, Crossing, Training

Chapter One

Soon after World War I began in August 1914, many young Americans—the idealistic, the patriotic, the restless, the adventuresome—found ways to participate without giving up their American citizenship. A small number went to the French Foreign Legion. Larger numbers, mainly college students, went to drive ambulances for the American Ambulance Service and Norton-Hartjes Service. Within the period of American neutrality, many pro-Ally preparedness programs were developed. A leading example was the Plattsburg Camp concept, in which men learned the military basics in five weeks of instruction. The program boomed after the sinking of the *Lusitania* in 1915. By 1916, Regular Army officers at a dozen Plattsburg-type camps had given instruction to some sixteen thousand young business and professional men. During this period, college boys were, in the main, staying on campus.

Two unlikely and probably unpredictable trends led young Texan Brannen to enlist in the Marine Corps for land combat in Europe. First was a new attitude on American college campuses. Once the indecision was over and war was declared, there was a remarkable exodus into uniform; enlisting was the proper thing to do. Second was a dramatic, opportunistic expansion of the Marine Corps. While the small military service historically had responded to limited disturbances in out-of-the-way places, now its civil-military leadership was able to secure an assignment in land combat in Europe.[1]

America's declaration of war on April 6, 1917, was followed on May 18 by a manpower draft, the Selective Service Act, which authorized the United States president to raise five hundred thousand men immediately.[2] Masses of American college students, including graduate students, rushed into uniform. In his opening chapter, C. A. Brannen describes his own reasons for leaving Texas A&M while he was a nineteen-year-old sophomore.

The United States Marine Corps (USMC) in 1914 totaled fourteen thousand men. The fact that the corps expanded to over seventy thousand by the end of 1918 can, according to Marine Corps historian Jack Shulimson, be credited to the political ability of Maj. Gen. Commandant George Barnett. We are inclined to add that he was energetically supported by Secretary of the Navy Josephus Daniels and his remarkable, free-swinging assistant, Franklin D. Roosevelt.[3]

In 1914, the small Marine Corps became involved—and somewhat overcommitted—in carrying out President Woodrow Wilson's policy in Latin America. A brigade-sized landing at Veracruz, Mexico, was followed by a similar landing in Haiti and Santo Domingo in 1915. Barnett had the acumen to convince Daniels that the marines had a proper role in France. He proposed that the marines serve with the army, since the war largely would be confined to land and the president had the right, by law, to place any part or all of the Marine Corps under the War Department. Besides all that, Barnett wrote, "We had used the slogan 'First to Fight' on our posters and I did not want that slogan made ridiculous."

Barnett, acting with and through Roosevelt and Daniels, persuaded Secretary of War Newton Baker to accept a brigade of marines, specified for a combat role, to sail with the first contingent of troopships. As the first portion of the promised brigade, the 5th Marine Regiment was under canvas in France by July 23, 1917, and began training in the company of the army's 1st Division. The 6th Marine Regiment began arriving in September, and the marine brigade was formed within the army's 2nd Division. The last elements of the 6th Marines arrived in France in February 1918.

During this very period, C. A. Brannen, who eventually would join these 6th Marines, resigned from Texas A&M College in January 1918, at the end of his fall semester. By February 11, he had been sworn into the Marine Corps at Parris Island, South Carolina. Brannen's transition from college student to marine rifleman is the subject of the first chapter of this book. Marines don't forget boot camp.

When America declared war in 1917, I was a few months past eighteen years of age and just finishing my first year in college. By the time I was to reenter in the fall for the second year, war activities were [proceeding] on a large scale. Men were going into some branch of the service on all sides. I felt that my family should do their bit in uniform, and my age designated me as the most appropriate one. With this decision behind, the next was selecting a branch of service. The aviation corps was the first choice, but in my mind there was the danger of never qualifying as a pilot, so I took second choice, the Marine Corps. The "First to Fight" recruiting posters were appealing. Accordingly, I joined the exodus from Texas A&M College, as cadets went into different branches of service. My resignation was January 27, 1918, at midterm.[4]

I was sworn into service at Parris Island, South Carolina, February 11, 1918. The camp, out on an island, was uninhabited except by soldiers and a few Negroes, and since a "boot" had no privileges, contact with the outside world was broken, except for mail.

The system used in drilling recruits was for an expert drill master to take about forty men and train them in close order drill. Expert rifle and pistol shots helped instruct on the range in the latter part of the training, but the drill sergeant had charge until we left this camp at the end of about two and one-half months. The drill sergeant bore down in order to show us what little we knew of military affairs, and in my case he succeeded admirably. My military training in college helped me over many rough places in one way and was a hindrance in others. Any movement which had been slighted before had to be done with precision now. Sergeant Boynton, my drill master, was satisfied with nothing short of perfection. He flew into a rage at one time and broke his swagger stick into several pieces because we were not doing as well on the drill as we should. Many times the air almost turned blue with the things he said. There was an order which kept a recruit from being cursed directly, but he caught it indirectly. A young fellow such as I was made

Cadet Carl Brannen, Texas A&M University, 1916 or 1917.

to feel that he was no earthly good to his nation and the sooner he got cut down on the front line the better off the country would be.

We did all of our own housekeeping. Each one helped at the kitchen periodically except when he was punished by doing extra duty. We washed our own clothes and sewed them when necessary. Among my washing one day was a pair of socks which my brown shoes had stained. I scrubbed and scrubbed, but the stain remained. When our washing was inspected, Sergeant Boynton's helper, a corporal from Massachusetts, knocked my wash in the dirt because he thought the socks were not clean and ordered me to wash them over. He took the attitude that I had not tried to wash them good. I almost forgot the ordeal of a court-martial and waded into him, but a breach of discipline in training camp would have carried a severe penalty. I was conscious of the necessity of this training, but it was much worse than [I had] expected.

When orders came that we were to be moved to make way for a new group of recruits, the boys got together and by each contributing about fifty cents, a nice little cash present was made up for Sergeant Boynton and his helper. I regretted the part of mine which went to the helper.[5]

The sergeant lined us up before our barracks the last time and told us that we were well-drilled marines and would have spoken further, but stopped and turned his back. We understood and saw him through blurred eyes as we moved off to catch the train and he sadly took up another bunch of boots. I heard that he finally succeeded in getting transferred to France and never survived the war.[6] We stopped some time in Florence, South Carolina, and I'm sure that if our recent instructor could have seen us swinging through the streets on parade in perfect time to the music, he would have been proud of his work. We were sent to the Marine Camp at Quantico, Virginia, near Washington, where a battalion was assembled for overseas. Some of the battalion came from the battleship *Tennessee*. In a few more days we arrived at Philadelphia, marched through to the strains of "Over There," and embarked on the transport *Henderson*.[7] Five hundred sailors were aboard, going to France to man the big naval guns to be used for bombarding purposes.[8] We were stuffed in like sardines, but I happened to get a hammock hung from the ceiling out on deck. I got seasick the first day by the time we were out of sight of land down Delaware Bay, and remained sick and miserable the entire thirteen days crossing. The ship was kept in complete darkness at night, as a light would have betrayed us to any submarine nearby. Each fellow wore a life preserver at all times, and they were somewhat uncomfortable to work and sleep in. One night one of the cannons fired, and we were immediately ordered out on deck. They thought a submarine was trying to torpedo us and we would have to leave the ship if it started sinking.

There were five or six ships in our convoy, all painted in the striped camouflage color. I don't see how they kept from running into each other at night, but each morning they would be about the same distance apart. My job on the ship was to stand watch in the steering room certain hours each day so we could keep the ship on its course by hand if the electrical apparatus went wrong.

No one was allowed to throw anything over in the water because it would get the whales or fish to following the ship and a submarine might pick up the trail from them. The garbage was collected and thrown over at one time. When [we arrived] in the real submarine zone near Europe, orders went out that if anyone fell overboard, the ship would not stop to pick them up. I watched my step around the rail. In one of the storms the waves were rolling so high that they came over my deck spraying everything, creating the danger of my being washed overboard.

As soon as our boat docked, we were put to work unloading it. The sailors and marines worked in relays. From among the boxes of canned goods being loaded for the crane, I picked up an odd-shaped box which I set out on the dock with the rest. Imagine my astonishment a few minutes later when a big naval officer dashed down in the hold where we were and wanted to know who sent that box up. He said that it contained enough nitroglycerine to blow up Brest Harbor. No one said a word, but I had a mental picture of its being thrown around up there with the other boxes.

When the ship was unloaded, we struck out for the Napoleon barracks five miles away. The barracks were some old stone buildings which the emperor had used to house his soldiers, but we used our tents. It was warm during the day and cold and disagreeable at night, but anything was better than the unbearable crowded condition of the boat. The hike after being cooped up caused the soles of my feet to become so sore I could scarcely bear to put them to the ground. But it was up early and work or drill all day while we were there and drag off dog-tired to bed at night to shiver in the cold, even though it was the first part of May. We evidently were the first troops to begin this camp. A year and a half later when I returned, it was scarcely recognizable. The camp then had the capacity for handling several thousand soldiers comfortably at one time.

At the end of a week, we received our first ride on a French troop train. The capacity of these cattle cars were forty men or eight horses. It would be horses one trip and maybe men the next. There was room for the forty to sit in the boxcar, provided each one drew his legs up under his chin and slept by leaning over on someone else. Usually there was a layer of straw on the floor, which helped some. It was hard to choose which was worse, the ship or the boxcar. The advantages with the latter were that a stop was made two or three times a day and the men were allowed to stretch their legs, and no train ride lasted over two or three days. Besides the discomfort of both modes of travel, there was the danger of being torpedoed out of the water in one case and bombed from the air in the other.

During this ride, our train stopped in a railroad yard alongside a flat car with a big barrel of wine on it. Some of the men pried around the big peg in the barrel until it came out, and along with it came a stream of wine. There was a mad scramble out of the cattle cars, all with cups and canteens ready. Soon the wine was ankle deep on the ground, so that some of the men began getting it there. The officers, riding comfortably and uncrowded in the better cars apart from the men, soon found out what was going on back down the line, but most of us got back in our cars by the time they arrived. Those men who were so far gone on the wine that they could not make it back to the cars, and did not care either, were court-martialed. They did time under guard and had part of their pay deducted. Another time, at a stop a soldier bought a quart of wine from a Frenchman, but an officer saw him and took the bottle and broke it on the track. Discipline was strict, and nothing was to interfere with the Americans' training. After the newness of being in France wore off, there were not so many restrictions about drinking when off-duty and back from the line.

From Brest we went diagonally across France to an obscure place in the southeastern part near the Swiss border.[9] At Dijon we ate a meal of white bread, the last for many of us. Because of America's unprepared condition, we were now eating French rations of brown bread and the so-called monkey meat from South America.

Those among us designated as machine gunners were issued French Chau Chau's.[10] The riflemen still had the good old American-made Springfields. These Springfields were not only excellent shooting irons, but good for close quarters and bayonet fighting.

In this mountain camp, the final touches were put on for the front lines. Most commands were executed at the double, meaning it was executed at a run. The drill ground was the flat top of

"It would be horses one trip and maybe men the next. There was room for the forty to sit in the boxcar, provided each one drew his legs up under his chin and slept by leaning over on someone else." These marines seem resigned to their rough accommodations. Photo No. 127-G-520934, National Archives, Washington, D.C.

a high hill. It was up before daylight, a hurried breakfast, a little while to police up quarters, and then the man-killing ascent to the top of the hill. We reached the drill ground exhausted, but there were only a few minutes to blow, followed by hours of hard training. In addition to the other drill, I found out all about my machine gun. I could take it apart and reassemble it blindfolded. This was necessary in order to be able to repair the machine gun in the dark if it should jam on the front line.[11]

Belleau Wood

Chapter Two

C. A. Brannen, having come through the personnel pipeline from his Parris Island training days, now arrives at his combat assignment. Going "up front" to join a rifle company of the 6th Marine Regiment, in the army's 2nd Division, he arrives two days after the violent beginning of the action that has gone down in American military history—and especially in Marine Corps history—as Belleau Wood. Here we pause to sketch Brannen's new world, his arena of action.

In the American Expeditionary Forces (AEF), a combat division—at 28,000 men almost double the size of French and British divisions—was organized with four army regiments formed into two brigades.[1] Twenty-nine such divisions fought in combat before the armistice was signed on November 11, 1918. The 2nd Division, however, was unique in having its 3rd Brigade consist of the U.S. Army's historic 9th and 23rd Infantry Regiments, while the 4th Brigade was formed from the U.S. Marine Corps' 5th and 6th Regiments. Historian S. L. A. Marshall called them "a little raft of sea soldiers in an ocean of Army."[2] Moreover, in these days of combat, the "Marine Brigade" was commanded by the army's Brig. Gen. James Harbord, who recently had been chief of staff to AEF Commander-in-Chief John J. Pershing. As Harbord departed for his assignment on May 5, the formidable

Pershing cheered him with: "I'm giving you the best brigade in France, and if things don't work out I'll know who to blame."[3]

Marines in an army division? Yes, indeed. When the United States had declared war on April 6, 1917, Franklin D. Roosevelt, then assistant secretary of the U.S. Navy, was instrumental in insuring that marine combat units were represented in the ground war in France. Thus, when the army's 1st Division was hastily formed and sent to France as a token for faltering Allies, the 5th Marine Regiment was dispatched at the same time and initially trained with the 1st Division. After the 2nd Division's headquarters was formed in October, the 5th Marines joined the army's 9th and 23rd Infantries. Filler units, including successive elements of the 6th Marine Regiment, arrived until the division was complete in February 1918.[4] In this chapter, Brannen describes his arrival in the combat area and his assignment to the 6th Marines.

Across many years and wars, when a soldier is asked "What happened?" he will begin his reply with, "Well, me and my buddy were—" So many times, "me and my buddy." Brannen's new world began with the "pals" within his dozen-man squad and then expanded to include his sixty-man platoon commanded by a lieutenant, his company of some 250 men commanded by a captain, and his battalion of about a thousand men commanded by a major. Brannen slowly learned about the people at battalion command, but he shows little concern for the leadership at the remote regiment, brigade, and division levels, where unknown senior persons daily made decisions that ultimately determined who lived and who died. For people in a rifle company, in any war, those higher echelons collectively are called "the rear-area bastards" or worse, and such a bastard is defined as "anybody whose foxhole is behind mine."

The Germans knew in the spring of 1918 that the war had to be won on the Western Front in the summer of 1918, before blockades strangled their country and before the Americans' rapidly increasing combat power could be applied. The March 21 offensive was the first of five. Young Brannen came to the front at the most dramatic and critical stage of the third offensive, which began on May 27. In the developing crisis, the AEF Commander-in-Chief, Gen. John J. Pershing, on March 28 had offered French Marshal Foch "all that we have," which at that time was just four combat-ready divisions—the 1st, 2nd, 26th, and 42nd.

As the Germans continued their phased offensives, the Americans—now 650,000 strong—were still holding "quiet fronts," but the 1st Division had conducted the first American offensive, a meticulously planned and rehearsed attack beginning on May 28, to reduce a small salient at Cantigny. This success was upstaged, however, as the Germans had initiated their third offensive on the previous day. Forming along the east-west ridge of the historic Chemin des Dames, north of and paralleling the Aisne River, the Germans on that first day gained an area twelve miles deep and thirty miles wide at the top, running almost to Reims to encompass the transportation complex at Soissons. By May 30, the Germans were on the Marne at Château-Thierry, some fifty miles from Paris.

With the U.S. 1st Division extending its defensive line in the Cantigny area, the 2nd Division and the new 3rd Division were now sent to blunt the south end of the salient. Advance elements of the 3rd Division met the Germans in the streets of Château-Thierry on May 31, then came back across the Marne to resist all German efforts to make a bridgehead there. Just to the west, the 2nd Division replaced retreating French forces, and here began the lengthy battle now known as "Belleau Wood." It consisted of a defensive phase between May 31 and June 5 and then an offensive phase that lasted from June 6 through June 26. The June 6 Marine attack took, at enormous cost, the key terrain at Hill 142 and the town of Bouresches, but it gained only a foothold along the southern edge of Belleau Wood.

The initial objective for the 2nd Division was to take back from the Germans the critical terrain features of Hill 142, the village of Bouresches, and the large dark mystery of Belleau Wood. Brannen would arrive on June 8, and what followed is the subject of this chapter.[5] Just prior to his arrival, however, the following battlefield events took place.

June 6, Morning: Under command of French XXI Corps, the 2nd Division began a series of costly attacks that eventually would clear Belleau Wood and the town of Vaux. On this first morning, the 1st Battalion, 5th Marines, under Maj. Julius Turrill, led with an attack across wheat fields that led to the capture of Hill 142. This action was preliminary to an attack on the mass of Belleau Wood, directly to the east and supposedly held only thinly by the Germans.

June 6, Afternoon: At 5 P.M., Maj. Benjamin Berry's 3rd Battalion, 5th Marines, and Maj. Berton Sibley's 3rd Battalion, 6th Marines, moved in neat skirmish lines toward the southern portion of Belleau

Wood. The woods contained an entire German regiment. The attackers were able to cling to a forward edge of the wood. Also at 5 P.M., the 79th Company and the 96th Company of Maj. Thomas Holcomb's 2nd Battalion, 6th Marines (to which Brannen was assigned two days later and which nominally was in a support position), made a violent, headlong attack on Bouresches. After the 96th Company's Capt. Donald F. Duncan was killed by a Maxim bullet in the stomach, 2nd Lt. Clifton B. Cates went into the village with about thirty men and held it until help arrived.[6] From this small action emerged two future commandants of the Marine Corps: Battalion Comdr. Thomas Holcomb became commandant in 1936, and platoon leader Clifton Cates assumed that position in 1947.[7]

The one day of June 6 had cost the marines, in killed or wounded, mostly in the rifle companies, total casualties of thirty-one officers and 1,056 men. Belleau Wood was not cleared until twenty days later. Add to that grim highlight the brighter fact that, beginning on this day, the American public knew, through a censorship lapse, that these specific Marine Corps units were fighting, while no army units could be identified. The break came because news correspondent Floyd Gibbons, before he left to accompany Major Berry in the assault, made a preliminary filing: "I am up front and entering Belleau Wood with the U.S. Marines." When Berry was hit, Gibbons attempted to help and was himself hit three times, one bullet destroying his left eye. A censor, feeling sympathetic because he heard that Gibbons had been killed outright, decided to clear the field release, and headlines in American papers blossomed: "U.S. Marines Smash Huns," "Marines in Great Charge Overthrow Crack Foe Forces." Historian Robert Moskin observes that "by such a fluke came glory!" The incident also initiated "smoldering resentments" of long duration on the part of the as-yet-unpublicized army.[8]

June 7: No major attacks were mounted this day. Lines were adjusted. Holcomb's 2nd Battalion, 6th Marines, spent the day dodging bullets while building up protection of the lodgement at Bouresches.

June 8: The day of Brannen's arrival and assignment to 80th Company. Before he arrived, that company under Capt. Bailey M. Coffenberg was attached to Sibley's 3rd Battalion for a 5 A.M. attack that stalled after two hundred yards against the scything of Maxim machine guns. At 3 P.M., the troops were withdrawn with heavy losses.

In a company history written in 1919, Lucian H. Vandoren reports:

> We made our objective [German machine-gun nests] but because of the lack of reinforcements were ordered to fall back. The position was taken by bayonet charge, with a loss of three lieutenants killed: Lieutenant C. A. Dennis, J. S. Timothy, and C. H. Ulmer; three lieutenants wounded: J. C. Cogswell, H. D. Shannon, and T. E. Whiting, and twenty-one men killed, eighty-three wounded, one prisoner of war, and one missing.[9]

We were in a peaceful little village eight miles from a railroad. One day when it was my time to work in the village at camp instead of drilling, we were digging a ditch and, in order to get through a rock, a grenade was touched off. After the explosion, the French nearby began running around in circles scanning the sky and saying *Boche*, their name for a German. They thought at first that a plane was bombing us.

On the Western Front, the Germans, having brought their troops from the Eastern Front, who had been used against Russia, were steadily advancing. They were shelling Paris with the Big Bertha. Some American Regulars, two or three divisions of National Guard, and a brigade of marines had been in France for several months and had been on the line in sections where no active fighting was being done during late winter and early spring. The brigade of marines, with two brigades of Regulars, made up the 2nd Division, which was a unit of 28,000 men commanded by Major General Harbord.[10] My battalion of a thousand men was used as replacements for the Marine Brigade of the 2nd Division.

The German drive had been on since March 21. General Haig had issued his famous "Back to the Wall" order for the British, and the French were exhausted. Conditions became so critical in the face of the enemy advance that the Allies laid aside all differences and united under one commander, the French General Foch, for the first time in the war. The French and English did not expect the Americans to be of much help at the front, as they felt that inexperienced troops could not hold where veterans had failed. However, the news came into our camp from British wounded that the Americans should be put in, to see what they could do.[11]

One night about nine o'clock, sometime after the first of

June, we were ordered to pack and be ready to leave right away. None of us knew where we were going, but at the appointed time every man was on the road with his pack containing everything he possessed and with his rifle in his hand. We swung off into the black night, headed for our railroad station. We reached it near daybreak, tired but glad for any kind of change. We had come to accept the condition of being tired and hungry as an almost continual feeling. Our train traveled all day in a northern direction, and that night when it stopped we could hear a distant rumble, which was the bombardment at the front. The next day we passed villages where the houses showed effects of shell and machine-gun fire. That evening we passed through the suburbs of a large city which we recognized as Paris, from the Eiffel Tower which reached over nine hundred feet into the air. Next came St. Denis and Meaux. At the latter place, we left the train, since that was as close as a train dared go to the front, and got on trucks.

Our trucks traveled toward Metz, a German city at that time, on the Paris-Metz Highway, which crosses the Marne River at the city of Château-Thierry. We were going toward the hottest part of the front, where the Germans had whipped all opposition to the spearhead of their drive for Paris. This great French highway was crowded with the American troops going toward the front and the civilian population fleeing in the opposite direction. A few civilians would remain with their homes and take chances with the German occupation, but most of them fled. There was danger of being killed when much fighting took place right at one's home. That evening we viewed many a sad face, with tragedy written in every line, going in the opposite direction. They kept well over on the side or completely off the road so as not to impede our progress. There were old people and children traveling by different conveyances. Only the crippled and very young children would be riding on household goods and valuables which were not to be left for the enemy.

We rode fifteen or twenty men per truck and had standing room only. There were about sixty trucks, for our battalion stretched out for over half a mile. The only French soldiers I saw were some on the ridges around Meaux who were feverishly digging a network of trenches out across the wheat fields. Of course the young wheat, about half knee high, was suffering from the depredations. I was told later that the American commander was ordered to contact the enemy and retreat [in] as orderly [a manner] as possible back to the trenches, where both forces would try to make the last stand that side of Paris. His reply was, "Retreat, hell! We just got here!"[12]

We were unloaded near the front and lay down beside the road with our packs on. By this time we were used to keeping on our clothes all the time and eating when there was anything to eat. The clothes kept off the cold at night, and you were always ready to move at a moment's notice. During the night, a train of trucks with provisions for the front stopped along beside us, and some men were able to get a few loaves of bread before being stopped. After daylight, a number of ambulances sped by, each one loaded down, going to the hospitals in Paris. The Americans had met the Germans with a deadly machine-gun fire at Château-Thierry, while the marines made a stand northwest of the city outside of Belleau Wood. On June 6 they attacked the strong Belleau Wood position. It was now the day after that and the wounded were being evacuated.[13]

My battalion was scattered out among the two marine regiments which were on the front to take the place of the killed and wounded. On June 8th about fifteen of us were attached to the 80th Co., 6 Reg.[14] This company had only about eighty men left out of the two hundred and fifty that made the attack. Captain Coffenberg had been wounded and Captain Lloyd, who had commanded me since we left Virginia, became captain.[15] The first day, while we were lying in support just back of the front, one of the new men near me shot the trigger finger off his right hand.[16] I never had anything make me jump any worse than when his gun went off right behind me.

We lay in our foxholes for protection against the shrapnel for a few days, being careful to stay hidden when German planes flew over looking for targets for their shells.[17] We then took over a company's place on the line, while they lay in support for us. If the enemy captured the first line position, he would be against another right behind it, while still further back there was another line of reserve troops. The shifting of the men from position to position, or from the front, depended on how badly they had fared. A narrow tongue of a rocky wooded ridge about thirty feet wide and a hundred yards long jutted out into a wheat field. Across the field a short ways on either side and in front was another rocky wooded ridge or ravine. This tongue

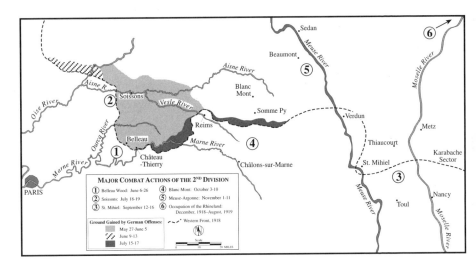

Map 1. Major Combat Actions of the 2nd Division. Map by Rolfe L. Hillman, Jr.

of timber was my first front line position. Belleau Wood was probably a mile square, with irregular patches of land here and there in cultivation.

By this time we had thrown away all of our pack, including extra underwear, a shirt, toothbrush, razor, etc. Crossing an open space must be done at full speed in order to make as poor a target as possible. There might be bayonet fighting at close quarters when there was no more time to load, and one could not afford to be hampered with excess weight. The only thing one should carry was food, if any, and ammunition. They were firing on us from three sides with one-pounders, rifles, and machine guns—some initiation for an inexperienced front-line man. They made a raid on us the first night, and I pumped so many bullets through my rifle that the barrel was too hot to hold. We sent up flares which showed them to us like we had been shown the night before while making relief.

I had been so horrified at the death, destruction, and danger on all sides that I had forgotten about my stomach. During the lull in watching the next day, I thought of my last meal behind the lines, when the cook told us to take some extra steaks which were cooked and save them for a later need. Mine had a greenish look to it, but was eaten with relish. Then I realized how thirsty I was.

Carl Brannen spent his first night with the 80th Company somewhere near these ruins of Bouresches, 1918. Photo is reversed. Photo No. 519175, National Archives, Washington, D.C.

A half-mile off and just inside our lines was the village of Bouresches, the only water supply in that vicinity. Lieutenant Robbinson [*sic*] with twenty-five men of the 96th Co. had charged through the streets and captured it in the general attack.[18] Since it was uncertain when water could be gotten, I gathered up the canteens from my nearest companions and wormed my way down just behind the lines toward the well. There were woods of shattered trees for protection until I was within two hundred yards of the well.

As I went this route, the realities of war were exposed at their worst. Bodies of men, most of them killed three or four days before, were scattered in all directions, lying as they fell. One could not have recognized his own brother, since their faces had turned black. Possibly their knapsacks had been searched by the men nearest them for any food they might have had. Since I was so thirsty, the thought struck me, why not carry two canteens. All Americans carried the same size canteens, but the German officer carried a larger one than the common soldier, with a cloth fitting skintight around it and a strap to carry it around your shoulder. I selected one of that kind on a dead officer and carried it with me.

At the edge of the wood, I paused to speak to a group hold-

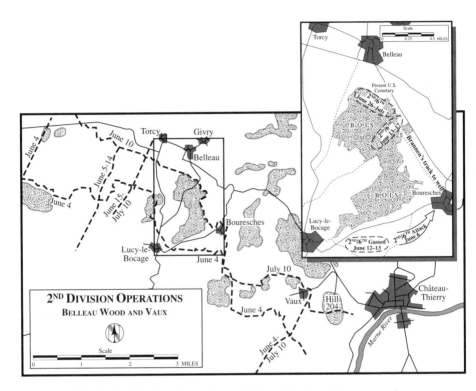

Map 2. 2nd Division Operations at Belleau Wood and Vaux, June 5–July 5, 1918. Maps by Rolfe L. Hillman, Jr., and Peter F. Owen.

ing a position. "Get your head down, Greeny," one said in a low quick voice.[19] I obeyed instantly and missed a volley. At the edge of the opening, I got on my stomach and crawled through the young wheat to the village.

The houses were razed, but when shelling began, I would run in a cellar. They were trying to hit our well and cave it in, apparently, for I had to run two or three times before getting all the water I wanted and filling my canteens. The wool cloth had closed back over a bullet hole through the German officer's canteen, and it was useless.

The return trip was made the same way. When we were relieved, I had been on the front three days without batting an eye. Troops left the front line with a haggard, worn look on their faces.

One night not very long after this, we were lying in our foxholes near the front and a runner brought word that help was needed at the front line.[20] The Germans were breaking through. The night was inky black, and I had taken off my wrapped leggins [*sic*] and had to crawl around feeling for them under the heels of some artillery horses tied right by me and almost got my brains kicked out. I decided right then that I would never pull off anything at night again. I just had time to get my leggins in my pocket and move off with the line.

The guide moved off with a man right behind holding onto his pack with one hand, another held onto the second, and so on through the woods in single file. The guide was supposed to know the best route for the least shelling. It did not matter if it was across ravines, over boulders, and across timber felled by the shells and machine-gun fire.

We had gone just a short ways when there was a terrific gas shelling. It does not take long to tell the difference in the sound of the explosion of a gas, shrapnel, or high explosive shell. Every man immediately stopped, put on his gas mask, and then continued the journey. The mask is uncomfortable at any time and especially when you are perspiring from exertion, with the rubber mask air tight over your face. If it is daytime, the lens clouds up on the inside and you can't see. We got out of the gas area with plenty of stumbling along and found things not quite as critical at the front as was expected.

At other times we lay for hours in our foxholes with masks on. There was no breeze on the hot June nights to carry the gas away through the foliage. One day my nearest companion, Becker, brought his canteen to his mouth, brushing it against some foliage where the gas had settled, burning his tongue and lips.[21] The inside of my nostrils stayed raw for several days from breathing the gas from the high-explosive shells. Scratches on your body were kept irritated by the gas, and where the pack rubbed your shoulders it would burn. The Germans could not retake our part of the woods by attacking, so they were trying to gas us out. Whenever a shell hit directly under a man, he would be hurled into the air and rain down in pieces. Slivers of flesh would go some distance.

The most optimistic person I ever saw was Lieutenant Cates of the 96th Company in our battalion. In one of the gas attacks his entire command was wiped out, and he was attached to my group until more men could be brought for him to command.[22] With his winning personality, he was able to cheer us when

"The most optimistic person I ever saw." 2nd Lt. Clifton B. Cates of 96th Company. Argonne, Fall 1918. Photo No. 127-G-515351, National Archives, Washington, D.C.

everything looked as dark as it possibly could. His lion courage in the face of any danger was enough to bolster one's morale. I hated to see him leave us.

The lieutenant in command of my platoon, Johnny Overton, had a slender athletic body.[23] In the spring of 1917, he was captain of Yale University's track team and held the American record for the mile run. Johnny was a he-man through and through. Our casualties were so heavy in going to or from the lines in large groups that the plan was hit upon to come off in small groups and reassemble at some appointed place. This plan was all right when you had been on one front long enough to know the territory well. It did my heart good to follow Overton. His torrid pace didn't seem bad going away from the front.

During the nights on the front, we stood in our trench watching without ever sleeping. Some sleepyheads would dose off

2nd Lt. John Megan Overton. Near the Marne,
July 1918. Photo No. 127-G-518352, National
Archives, Washington, D.C.

now and then, while in the daytime most of us would catnap. I
never slept at night and for only a few minutes at a time during
the day. The times I carried a rifle with the bayonet on it instead of a machine gun, I could set the butt on the ground and
the end of the bayonet reached to my chin. When I was so
sleepy that I would start to sink down from a standing position
the bayonet would pierce my chin and arouse me. During the
long hours of night at "stand to," you would think of everything in the world.

At one time my trench faced a young peach orchard out in
no man's land. The trees were spaced evenly to resemble men
in attack formation; more than once while it was breaking day
and light enough to show their forms, I would get over my gun

with fingers on the trigger and ready to begin mowing down men when it would dawn on me about the orchard. The attack was always made at daylight by either side, and that was about the most nervous time of the day. When we captured a new position, the first thing was to fortify it as much as possible against attack. One night a number of four-foot stakes sharpened at one end were brought us with a spool of barbed wire. I was sent out with the detail to put up the wire in front of our trench. The fellow holding the stake while another drove it in the hard ground with the maul was in danger of having his hands hit or maybe even hit across his tin hat. This had to be done at night when the enemy could not see to shoot at you. When a flare was shot into the air, we hid as quickly as possible, but even at that there were always some being hit. After the stakes were set, we twisted the wire around among them, making a mass for our enemy to cross before getting on us. Some of our men back in the trenches thought the wire detail had returned to the trenches when we had not. Hearing us out there in the dark moving around, they thought it was a raiding party and opened fire. We only saved ourselves by dropping to the ground until they found out who we were.

A raid would be made now and then to get prisoners for questioning. This was to try and find out if there was anything out of the ordinary being planned by the opposite side. Another way to find out if preparations were being made under cover of darkness on the other side was for two or three men to slip over near the enemy trench and hide behind something and listen. If you made any noise like stepping on a stick and breaking it, you had better hide quickly or run like everything, because they would send up a flare, making things as light as day for a minute.

Food and water were brought to the front line once in twenty-four hours, at night, if the shelling didn't stop them. One morning the detail was so late that they arrived after daylight. Part of my company was out in a very exposed position. However, rather than see his men go without nourishment, Sergeant Willie went out with the food and water himself. Just as he reached the hole where they were, a bullet dropped him in with them. Word came back to where I was by the grapevine route that he was bleeding badly and something should be done to save him. Lieutenant Overton asked for volunteers. A fellow named Walker and I procured a stretcher and went out. We stood there in full view of the enemy trench for what seemed like an hour, when in reality it was only a minute, while he was passed up to us. We put him on the stretcher and walked off without being fired at directly, it seemed.[24] The Dutchmen could have taken aim and got both of us. As we went back through the woods, a shell hit close, but we jumped behind a tree with our stretcher, and no one was hurt badly. Walker received a gash across the back of one hand from the flying shrapnel but kept carrying his end of the stretcher. We reached a deep ravine behind the lines, where a first-aid station had been set up, and left our cargo. On the return to my place in line, I ran into an Austrian 88 Whizz Bang barrage. I jumped into the nearest hole, landing next to a fellow who had been dead several days. The scent was stifling, but I stayed with him until the firing settled down above me.

Belleau Wood was captured a piece at a time, and by the first of July it was all in the Americans' possession.[25] The Prussian Guards, the pick of Germany's troops, had been pushed back. They had us outnumbered in this forty days of fighting about three to five. We could tell from the numbers on the uniforms of the prisoners and dead and by talking with them what troops they were. The first prisoners, upon asking and being told we were Americans, refused to believe it, saying we were Canadians. They said that the Americans could not get through their submarines. Newspapers taken on the prisoners or in their trenches emphasized the German success considerably.

My last position on that front was facing the present American cemetery for that section of the country, where the American soldiers were taken from their first hurried burial places and placed in orderly rows.[26] While occupying this position, a companion and I were operating a machine gun down in advance of the remainder of the company. We sneaked down the wooded hill to this place in the edge of the woods at night, so our gun could cover the open level space in front if an attack was made on us. We laid our gun down and set to work digging a hole to be in when daylight came, intending to put our gun on the edge in front, pointing out through the brush. When we were almost through, we realized day would soon come and we had not gotten any food or water since the night before. My companion went back to see about it, while I finished the job. Just as it was light enough to see some little ways, I suddenly saw a German soldier walking diagonally toward me along a path which went out in the open about six or seven feet from me. He was carrying his rifle in his right hand at the balance, with the bayonet, of course. My absent companion had the only Colt .45 between the two of us, and the German was too close for me to make a dive for my machine gun. I stood there still as a mouse, with shovel in hand, and looked at every feature on this young man's face as he walked by without seeing me.

He had an athletic build, [was] nearly six feet tall, and weighed about one hundred and seventy pounds. I never told of this incident for fear of being reprimanded for not shooting him in the back as he walked away. I should have gotten my machine gun after he passed and tried to take him prisoner. I had instructions to keep this machine-gun nest well hidden, which made me reluctant about firing when the game was so small. Out in the open, he was shot at three or four times, fell once, and lost his rifle but got away apparently unhurt. I heard a sergeant later chiding his men for missing such a good shot.

A few days before the 4th of July, orders came that some of the men (except machine gunners) would go back to Paris and parade. That left me out. Upon their return they reported that they were almost mobbed by a thankful people, and the Americans were being given credit for saving Paris.[27]

This battle of Belleau Wood was not large, as far as numbers of men engaged was concerned, but it was a great moral victory for the Allied side. The Germans named the American marines "Devil Dogs." The French government changed the name of Belleau Wood to American Marine Wood.

We were relieved from the front by the 26th (Yankee Division) from the New England states, but remained at the Marne River in reserve until the night of the 16th of July. A long-range shell came our way occasionally at this place, ten or fifteen miles from the front, but otherwise it was peaceful.

We stayed in the French houses, as practically all of the inhabitants were gone. We washed our clothes in the river without soap and swam around while they dried. We also fished with hand grenades until the officers stopped us.

On the fifteenth, we stood by our guns ready, as the Germans were launching an attack trying to break through.

Soissons

Chapter 3

After the battle of Belleau Wood, Holcomb's 2nd Battalion, 6th Marines, moved behind the 26th Division lines to the area formerly occupied by 2nd Division headquarters at Montreuil-aux-Lions, ten miles west of Château-Thierry on Route 3. While they restored themselves personally and as a military unit, events were taking place that led to a climax in this war.

On July 18, the Aisne-Marne counteroffensive began with a main attack launched eastward by French XX Corps. That day became known in history as the "Turn of the Tide," because the Germans never later initiated an offensive operation. Brannen provides a short account of the experience of the 6th Marine Regiment on July 19.

On the first day, the 5th Marines and the 9th and 23rd Infantry of the 2nd Division attacked twice, gained some five miles, and by nightfall were exhausted. On the morning of July 19, the 6th Marines made the only attack in the division area. Launched at 8:30 A.M. from the division's south sector, the regiment moved from the protection of Vierzy Ravine eastward across level ground toward the road between the villages of Villemontoire and Tigny, just west of the Soissons—Château-Thierry highway. This supply route was vital to the Germans if they were to escape entrapment in the Marne salient. The attack stalled, still a few hundred yards short of the highway, at 10:30 A.M., and for the rest of the day the 6th Marines lay under fire in such holes as the men could find. The regiment was relieved and brought out in the darkness of the night of July 19–20.[1]

It is a basic principle in military science that, when an attacker moves forward well into enemy lines, forming a pouch in which his lines of communication and supply run down the middle, he is vulnerable to counterattack from one or both flanks. The German salient, with a primary line of communication running north-south down the Soissons–Château-Thierry Road, had now come to rest on the Marne River at Château-Thierry, in part because of the timely employment of the American 2nd and 3rd divisions. The French high command, recognizing a classic vulnerability, began planning such a counterattack in mid-June. Development of the plan was delegated to the French Tenth Army under Gen. Charles Mangin, a colorful, tempestuous veteran of French colonial wars who was, perhaps unfairly, known universally as "the Butcher."[2]

General Mangin, who, as commander of the French Tenth Army, was the architect of the plan for the counterattack beginning July 18, was noted for his ability to concentrate troops and deliver an effective surprise blow. He was also noted for his lack of caution. For a small-scale experimental strike on June 11, he had been assigned five divisions. On the afternoon of June 10, only one division was at hand, the second was just detraining, the third was expected during the evening, the fourth at midnight, and the fifth later still. He told Marshal Foch, "I shall attack tomorrow." And he did. For the concentration at Villers-Cotterêts, southwest of Soissons, he was doing the same thing on a larger scale, and he now had access to two long-awaited American combat divisions. When an American staff officer told him that some units could not be brought to the line at the proper time, he replied calmly that he would choose to go ahead without all the planned troops and support, rather than give up the vital element of surprise.[3]

From the point of view of the 2nd Division's commander, Major General Harbord, meeting Mangin's requirements for surprise assembly was of greatest concern:

> A division of twenty-eight thousand men . . . had been completely removed from the control of its responsible officers and deflected by marching and by truck through France to a destination unknown to any of the authorities responsible for either its supply, its safety, or its efficiency in the coming attack. They said the divi-

sion would undoubtedly be in place in the forest by Wednesday morning.

I doubted it and said so, and was reassured by many shrugs of French shoulders.[4]

On the night of July 17, with the last-minute arrival of so many elements assembling to make their move eastward through the Forest of Retz, striving to meet an attack hour of 4:35 A.M., a mammoth traffic jam of men and vehicles occurred. The difficulties of the night march, as described by Col. Paul Malone, who was commanding the division's 23rd Infantry, were included at length in General Pershing's memoirs:

> No more difficult circumstances could have confronted a command than . . . on the night of July 17th–18th. Without reconnaissance of any kind it was compelled to move through absolutely unknown terrain during a night which was intensely dark and rainy, to thread its way through a road blocked to a standstill with traffic of all kinds. . . . The troops actually ran to their destinations.[5]

And, of course, down at the level of the command of Brannen's 2nd Battalion, 6th Marines, a different view obtained. Maj. Robert L. Denig, who had returned from cross-assignment to an army regiment, was temporarily in command, while Major Holcomb was, in turn, filling in for Colonel Lee at regiment. By Denig's account, the trucks did not arrive until midnight on the night of July 16–17, had several troop casualties from German artillery en route, regained a lost convoy, and were, after twelve hours riding, dumped in a big field.

After a few hours rest, the march forward began: "It was hot as Hades and we had nothing to eat since the day before. We at last entered a forest; troops seemed to converge on it from all points. At ten that night, without food, we lay down in a pouring rain to sleep."[6]

At the end of this night of struggles, as the attack hour neared, the 9th Infantry was in its assigned place in the attack line, the 23rd Infantry arrived at 4 A.M., and the 5th Marines actually ran to cross the attack line. The 6th Marines, having been designated corps reserve, were still back in the woods, following the 5th Marines.

This plan had been developed for launch on July 18. In Mangin's mind, the key to success would be a hasty concentration of divisions, moving into their final positions at night to escape German aerial observation. Surprise would be vital; to that end, the usual preparatory artillery barrage would not take place. Mangin's main attack was assigned to Gen. Pierre E. Berdoulat's XX Corps, whose front-line divisions consisted of (north to south) the American 1st Division, the French 1st Moroccan Division, and the American 2nd Division. Brannen's report on Soissons begins on the night of July 16, when trucks arrived to carry the 80th Company to a destination that Brannen hoped would be a rest camp. Of course, it was not. Although it was of little immediate concern to Brannen and his company mates, on July 15 Brig. Gen. James Harbord, who had commanded the Marine Brigade during Belleau, had been promoted to command the entire division, with the rank of major general. Col. Wendell C. Neville replaced him as Marine Brigade commander. The battle south of Soissons would confirm that broad decisions made by army, corps, and division commanders, all justified under "the exigencies of the service," could lead to the utter devastation of the officers and men of regiments, battalions, and companies.

On the night of July 16, we gathered near the Marne River and ate supper. Soon after dark, trucks arrived to carry us back to a rest camp (we hoped) after five weeks in Belleau Wood, and everyone seemed in good spirits. There were not enough trucks, and my company had to wait until near day for some more to arrive. We rode nearly all day toward our unknown destination. By evening hopes of not going back to the front had about vanished. A straggler out of the First Division of Regulars caught my truck and rode a piece.

In the evening rather late, we were unloaded on the edge of Villers-Cotterêts forest and started toward the front about seven miles away. There seemed to be a general convergence of troops toward this forest, and the narrow graded road was inadequate for the traffic. To make matters worse, a rain had just fallen. In one place a tank had gotten ditched and caused a temporary holdup. We had to leave the road several times, all of which seemed to throw us behind some prearranged schedule. Delays caused worried looks to appear on the officers' countenances. Traveling through the dark forest at night was extremely difficult, and the fact that we had not eaten in twenty-four hours made it worse. We reached the front line exhausted but, without slowing up, immediately went into battle at daybreak. We reached the line just in time to go over the top at the zero hour.[7]

Our troops were playing the role of Stonewall Jackson's men (foot cavalry) in the Civil War. After forced marching and riding, a sudden, unexpected attack was being made. The prisoners captured, on being told we were American marines, said "No, the Marines are at Belleau Woods." Sometime during the day, I got about a spoonful of corned beef, which several of us divided. One of the men had gotten hold of a can somewhere and opened it with his bayonet.

The French cavalry with their long spears were back of us.[8] A division of Americans was on the right flank and a division on the left flank in the drive, while a division of Moroccans was attacking in the center. Much airplane fighting was going on, and several [planes] got shot down. A battle in the air is interesting, and we always watched them if we were not too closely occupied. We must have gained seven or eight miles that day, driving toward Rheims on the left flank of the Marne salient.[9] That night we stood by our guns to hold the gain, but we were tired and hungry.

The morning of July 19, the second day of the battle and the third day without food, we formed our lines in a road through a cut or ravine and came out for a charge across a sugar beet field.[10] The tanks were leading, with our lines right behind them. In trying to stop the charge, the Germans turned loose everything they had. It seemed to rain shells. One hit between me and the man on my left, Red Williams. It knocked a hole in the ground, half covered me with dirt, and left my hands and face powder-burned, but the shrapnel had missed. Red was not quite so lucky and received his death wound. I left him writhing and groaning on the ground to continue the attack.[11]

The last glance I had of Lieutenant Overton, he was walking backward and trying to shout something back to us. He carried his cane in the left hand and a .45 [pistol] in the right. The din and roar was so terrific that I didn't have any idea what he was saying, but interpreted it from his expression to be some words of encouragement. He was soon down, killed. The gunnery sergeant was killed.[12]

Just ahead of me, a few men grouped and started down a ditch. My training told me to keep out of groups, for a shell could kill several at one time. I leaped some barbed wire to the right of them as a shell hit, making a clean sweep. One of the men near me was shot through the shoulder; another had a finger shot off his hand. I opened our first-aid package and applied the gauze to the wound. They both left for the rear, hoping to make the hospital.[13] By this time, all of the tanks had been crippled or stopped and all the men around me shot down. I was now nearing the woods across the field in front of our attack zone. Realizing this, I began to look for a stopping place and found it in an old sunken road less than a foot deep. A volley from a machine gun missed me by inches, and, falling where I stood in the road, I drew fire which barely cleared my body for the rest of the day.

In thirty or forty minutes, our regiment had been almost annihilated. The field which had been recently crossed was strewn with dead and dying. Their cries for water and help got weaker as the hot July day wore on.[14]

There I was, under the enemy gun and almost in his lines by myself. I will never know how I went through that curtain of shells untouched. I was black from the powder of the exploding shells. Most of my trousers was left in the barbed-wire entanglements. At first I expected a counterattack and was prepared to come to my feet and sell myself as dearly as possible. The slaughter of my comrades had left a bad taste. The attack never came, but enemy planes flew low over the battlefield during the day and, as the pilot leaned his head over the side looking through his glasses, I lay feigning death. The hot sun made my thirst almost unbearable. A slug of shrapnel hit my foot, but the hobnails saved [me from] a serious wound.

Late in the evening, while I was wondering if I could get away after dark and contact any of my forces which were left, I saw an American uniform crawl across the road some hundred yards away. Laboriously crawling to where he disappeared, I found my old friend Lieutenant Cates of the 96th Company holding a trench with about twelve or fifteen men.[15] He asked me where the rest of the 80th Company was, and I told him that I didn't know, but thought most of them were hit. A dead German soldier was lying across the barbed wire in front of the trench. He was shot as he slowed up to cross. One of the men sneaked out and found a piece of black rye bread in his pack. I had a spoonful or two of sugar in my condiment can and with the sugar to sprinkle on the bread we got a bite around.

After midnight a force of Algerian troops came to relieve us, and gathering as many of our wounded as we could carry, we started back.[16] Three of us were carrying Cooper of my company in a blanket.[17] I was at the feet with the other two going

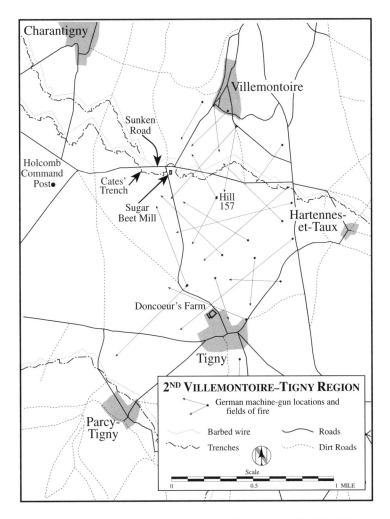

Map 3. 2nd Division Villemontoire–Tigny Region, July 19, 1918. Map adapted from Col. Loizeau, *Le combat d'une division*, Charles-Lavauzelle & Co.

ahead with the other end. Cooper was shot through the leg, arm, and head. We lost our hold on the blanket several times, letting him slip to the ground. Each time he greeted us with a groan. Finally we got back to a well, and I'm sure that I drank near a gallon of water within twenty minutes time. We went back a mile or two behind the lines and lay down.

The surviving marines who left the battle line were a terrible looking bunch of people. They looked more like animals. They had almost a week's growth of beard and were dirty and ragged. Their eyes were sunk back in their heads. There had been very little sleep or rest for four days and no food. Late in the evening of July 20, we survivors got a meal of slum gullion.[18]

One of our group related that while he was near an Algerian, he smelled a very offensive odor and upon investigation found him carrying a pouch with human ears in it. Some of the ears were pretty old. It was their custom to take the ears from the enemy they killed.[19]

There were so many wounded in the attack that the ambulance service broke down. Many were piled in trucks and jolted back over shell-torn roads, causing wounds which had become quite sore several hours after their infliction to start bleeding again. Gangrene caused other deaths when an early evacuation would have saved lives.[20]

The stretcher bearers all wore a Red Cross band around one arm to distinguish them from combatants, so they could go out in the open without being shot at. They never carried any arms. However, that branch of service suffered heavy casualties and had to keep giving first aid to the wounded and being subject to shell fire after the fighters dug in.

The battalion of four companies was put together, but that did not make one good-sized company. We lay down to rest near a battery of our artillery while food was being gotten ready. Soon sleep was interrupted by the boom of the battery sending a few shells over to Heinie. I was awakened suddenly by a fellow near me becoming a raving maniac. The strain had been too much and something had slipped in his head. Cases like this were called shell shock. We tried to reassure him that he was among friends away from the front, but he evidently thought he was in the middle of a terrible battle and surrounded by enemies. I dropped back down to sleep while he was being carried away.

An observation balloon was near the place where we were. A German plane dived and shot it down. The machine-gun bullets set fire to the balloon, but the observer came out in a parachute, landing in a tree.

The boys were more despondent than I ever saw them after this last battle, and no wonder. As far as I know, I was the only survivor of Overton's platoon of about fifty men.[21] There were eight able to walk away from the front, out of 212 on the com-

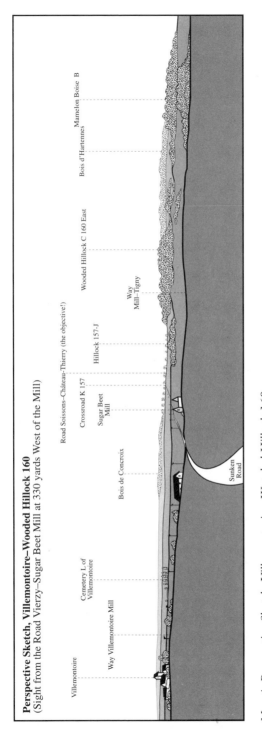

Perspective Sketch, Villemontoire–Wooded Hillock 160
(Sight from the Road Vierzy–Sugar Beet Mill at 330 yards West of the Mill)

Villemontoire

Cemetery L of Villemontoire

Way Villemontoire Mill

Bois de Concroix

Road Soissons–Château-Thierry (the objective!)

Crossroad K 157

Sugar Beet Mill

Hillock 157-J

Wooded Hillock C 160 East

Bois d'Hartennes

Mamelon Boise B

Way Mill–Tigny

Sunken Road

Map 4. Perspective Sketch, Villemontorie—Wooded Hillock 160, July 19, 1918. Map adapted from Col. Loizeau, *Le combat d'une division*, Charles-Lavauzelle & Co.

pany roster at this time. However, there were some fifteen or twenty men who claimed they got lost off during the night and were not in the terrible slaughter in the sugar beet field.[22]

By this time I had accumulated a good crop of cooties. I had been wearing the same clothes, day and night, for some months, wallowing in the dirt, and occupying the same place occupied by French colonial Negroes and other lousy troops. This body louse laid eggs in the seams of your clothes and multiplied pretty rapidly.

After moving away from the front, we came to a delouser. This was a boiler with a fire under it, in which your clothes were placed and steamed until the cooties were killed. While that was going on, we took a bath and put back on the same clothes. In a few weeks conditions would be just as bad again, necessitating another delousing. While you were in motion, you did not notice the cooties, but when you stopped, and especially when your body was wet with perspiration, their crawling around was most irritating. A tired and sleepy man would drop off to sleep in spite of them, though.

Gradually replacements were added, and the companies began to approach strength again. Some slightly wounded men had recovered and returned. Captain Coffenberg was among them, taking command of the company again. Within three or four weeks we had worked back to the front at Pont-a-Mousson. This was an inactive front, and since the strain and losses were not bad, we stayed about two weeks.[23]

St. Mihiel

As one of the first units to ship "over there," Brannen's 2nd Division had been one of the few combat-ready formations General Pershing could offer to the Allies during the crises of the summer. At both Belleau Wood and Soissons, Brannen and his fellow marines had fought under French generals.

But it had become a matter of both national pride and strategic interest for the United States to field its own army, under its own general. Americans quite naturally expected that their soldiers would serve under an American commander who would stand on an equal footing with his Allied counterparts. Furthermore, President Wilson had already begun to prepare his Fourteen Points, which would call for a League of Nations, a "peace without victory," and other ideas for postwar Europe. After four years of war, Great Britain and France might find Wilson's charitable ideas hard to swallow. An independent American army would strengthen Wilson's hand at the negotiating table. Therefore, for the AEF, making this army a reality became a strategic objective second in importance only to the defeat of the German army.[1]

This American army's first test would be to reduce the St. Mihiel salient, a quiet "bulge" southeast of Verdun. The salient had interrupted rail traffic between eastern France and Paris since the early days of the war.

Although the territory was lightly held and now considered indefensible by the German High Command, some Allied commanders openly questioned whether the inexperienced AEF staff was up to the task of taking it—and whether Pershing himself ever would be fully capable of directing an army. It was far better, they reasoned, to continue committing American divisions to the front under more experienced French and British corps commanders. A more extreme opinion expressed among ranking British officers called for dismantling American divisions into separate battalions, to serve in existing British brigades.[2] A successful prosecution of the St. Mihiel campaign would put an end to most of these arguments; a disaster might strengthen the AEF's critics and weaken America's stature among the Allies both for the duration and in the postwar negotiations.[3]

Although Ludendorff had decided to abandon the St. Mihiel salient, its defenses were not inconsequential. Since 1914, the Germans had fortified a defense, with row upon row of barbed wire, four to five zones deep. Two French offensives had failed to eliminate the salient early in the war; since then, it had evolved into a quiet sector. The German High Command rated the defending divisions as only second and third class. Eight and a half of these divisions, numbering slightly under a hundred thousand men, occupied a salient twenty-five miles wide and sixteen miles deep. The ground mostly consisted of open, gently rolling countryside, interrupted by occasional woods. As the 550,000 American and 110,000 French troops moved up to the front, marching by night and hiding in woods by day, a steady driving rain began. Temperatures dropped, misery increased, and the roads became a quagmire.[4]

As one of the few proven, experienced formations in the AEF, Brannen's 2nd Division figured prominently in the attack. Pershing committed his I Corps (including the 2nd Division) and his IV Corps to attack the southern face, while his V Corps, with one French and two U.S. divisions, would attack the west face of the salient. Gen. John A. Lejeune, the 2nd Division's commanding general, initially placed his 3rd Infantry Brigade in the lead and his 4th Marine Brigade behind them in support. Within the 4th Brigade, the 6th Marine Regiment would advance on the left, with the 5th Marines on their right. Taking up the rear of the 6th Regiment, the 2nd Battalion's companies formed on line, with each man in a file behind his squad leader. On paper, Brannen's battalion would be about two thousand meters behind the leading waves, with five thousand soldiers and marines between themselves and the German machine guns.[5] For once, the 2nd Battalion appeared to have drawn an easy assignment.

For Brannen and the 80th Company on September 12, St. Mihiel began as a walkover. The American attack providentially coincided with the beginning of a planned German withdrawal. The four-hour American barrage struck the defenders just as they had planned to pull out. Defending German infantry lost communication with their supporting artillery, and German commanders lost touch with their troops. Ahead of Brannen and the marines, the doughboys of the 3rd Brigade followed the barrage through the German outpost zone of machine-gun positions and over the main line of resistance, suffering light casualties. Barbed wire slowed the advance more than enemy fire. Nightfall found the 2nd Division twenty-four hours ahead of schedule.[6] It was an auspicious start for the first all-American offensive.

For the first three days of the offensive, Brannen and his battalion trailed behind the 3rd Infantry Brigade as it smashed through the German defenses. On September 15, the 2nd Battalion moved to the front in a poorly executed maneuver that has been largely ignored in the published histories of the marine units involved. As Brannen puts it, "My military sense didn't approve of what we were doing, but a soldier only obeys orders." By day's end, a great lapse in military judgment by officers who should have known better was evident.

Just after 2 A.M. on September 15, Col. Harry Lee, the 6th Marines' regimental commander, had ordered the 2nd Battalion to move north and occupy a line along the southern edge of the Bois de la Montagne. The 1st Battalion already had two companies on the northern edge of the wood. Lee did not intend this as an attack order, and he did not imply that resistance might be expected. It seems apparent that Colonel Lee intended for the 2nd Battalion simply to move forward and occupy a position which would provide a support line behind the two companies of the 1st Battalion.

The ensuing engagement graphically illustrates how a simple task can become hopelessly confused in the fog of battle. The Bois de la Montagne is a wood shaped like a W, roughly two kilometers wide. The top of the W is oriented to the northeast. The two companies (the 74th and 76th) of the 1st Battalion could never have defended the entire northern edge of the woods. Furthermore, these two companies had only been tasked with conducting a reconnaissance patrol; no unit yet had cleared the forest of Germans. In truth, the 74th and 76th had passed through the wood to its northeast corner, and these two companies now occupied positions 1,500 meters away from the point where Major Ernest C. Williams would enter the wood. To muddle the situation further, a morning ground fog had reduced visibility to 50 meters.

Despite the insistent pleadings of his scout officer, Major Williams led his battalion toward the Bois de la Montagne in a column of twos, with the 80th Company up front. Incredibly, Major Williams was so oblivious to the enemy threat that he rode at the head of his column on horseback. Just after dawn, as he turned the column off the main road to follow a ravine along the southern edge of the wood, the forest erupted with machine-gun fire from several directions.

The battalion immediately became disorganized and divided into two elements, one on either side of the Xammes-Charey Road. Brannen, in Kilduff's platoon, was caught in the initial barrage while crossing a small clearing on the west side of this road.

Despite the shock of the initial burst of fire, numerous casualties, and intense shelling, the marines recovered and formed a hasty defense along the unimproved road and in the woods southwest of the clearing. As the morning progressed, the 80th Company repulsed German counterattacks from two sides. Other companies came to their aid, attacked to the left and right, and eventually extracted the 80th Company from a very dangerous situation.[7]

Soon after being relieved, we began working our way toward the St. Mihiel salient by traveling at night and sleeping in woods or some hidden place during the day. There seemed to be a concentration of American troops moving toward this place from all directions. Word leaked out that General Pershing was expecting to have to pay 100,000 men for Metz, on from St. Mihiel, and one of the most strongly fortified cities in Europe.[8] This didn't sound like an exaggeration to me, for had not our gains in actual miles been small so far, at such losses? I heard that of the British Regulars rushed into France in 1914, there were very few left. So I reasoned that the war would continue a year or two longer, but that I would not see the finish.

Lieutenant Kilduff was now in command of my platoon.[9] He tried to drill us as much as possible with the idea in mind of keeping down so many casualties. Heretofore, we had come out of our trench or hiding place and rushed toward the enemy as fast as we could run, while they poured in a deadly fire with machine guns. What were left, if any, would go over the spouting machine guns and bayonet or shoot the gunners. Now we were to come out firing from the hip, which kept down the speed of advance, but we hoped to shoot them away from their guns before so much damage was done.[10]

The night of the 11th of September the rain came down in torrents, while there were continual flashes of lightning. This slowed up travel, and my command did not reach the trenches until after the barrage began. This was the first battle in which the Americans fought as a big unit themselves. At 2 A.M., the concentrated American artillery literally caused it to rain shells at the enemy front line and back across their reserve troops. So effective was this bombardment that the enemy artillery was scarcely able to answer. The roar and flashes were continual, and we stood almost waist deep in mud and water, shivering from our drenching, our excitement, and the cold wind which followed the rain.

At five o'clock, just as day was beginning to break, we came out of our trench and started across "No Man's Land" toward the enemy trenches. Our artillery lifted its range as we advanced and kept a line of shells bursting just ahead of us. This was the best artillery support our infantry had had up until this time and saved lots of casualties. We advanced about six miles by evening and entered the town of Thiaucourt.

That evening a fellow in the company named Musgrove pulled a fork out of his coat pocket. One of the prongs caught in the pin of a hand grenade in the same pocket, setting off the detonator. After pulling the pin you have five or six seconds to throw it before the explosion, just as a fire cracker after being lit. He was trying to get the grenade out of his pocket when the explosion occurred, killing him.[11]

Late in the evening of the first day, I found a lull in the fighting and made an assault on my cooties by burning them with my cigarette. A cigarette was the best friend a fellow had. On the front you had to get down under a blanket to light and smoke, with your hand covering the lighted stub. Bull Durham was the only kind we got to use, because it was issued out like rations. However, there were ready rolls available if you had the money. We got all we possibly could out of a cigarette before throwing it down. Then the French picked up the stubs and finished them when they were around.

One morning before daylight, the third or fourth day after the St. Mihiel battle began and before the lines had become adjusted again, Major Williams (who had succeeded Denig) led us forward in columns of squads.[12] My company, now under Captain Woodall because Coffenberg was wounded, was again leading, with my platoon leading the company.[13] My military sense didn't approve of what we were doing, but a soldier only obeys orders. Soon there was machine-gun fire from the well-known crack of German Maxims in our rear.

Just as it was breaking day, we unexpectedly came upon an enemy soldier beside the road and captured him before he could get away. Then the major halted and ordered Captain Woodall to send a platoon of his company ahead to reconnoiter. The captain sent Lieutenant Kilduff with about forty of us. When we were a hundred yards or so from the battalion and crossing an acre-sized clearing, we were fired upon by machine guns from the woods. Perhaps half of the platoon were shot down, including Kilduff. The rest of us dashed for the woods; those nearest brought the lieutenant, but a bunch of bullets had drilled a large hole in his left side. By this time it was a well-established fact that our battalion was surrounded, while the survivors of my platoon had the enemy on two sides and were almost cut off from the battalion.

My buddy at this time was Lewis Frillman, called Scatterbrain.[14] Just a few yards beyond the woods we entered was a bluff, and, looking over it, Scatterbrain discovered a large number of the enemy. Scatterbrain and I began on those over the bluff from us first. We were both rifle grenadiers at that time, with a cone to put the grenades in on the muzzle of our rifles. Each of us was carrying a pretty good supply. He had been wounded at Belleau Wood three months before, and this was his first battle since. He seemed determined to make up for lost time.

The boys over the bluff began to retreat under our fire, and we poured it on good and proper until they were out of sight over a ridge. In the retreat, two of them deliberately stopped, unfolded a blanket, rolled one of those who was down on it, and went carrying him off. Remembering my predicament at Belleau Wood with the wounded sergeant, I told Scatterbrain not to shoot at them. They got safely away with their wounded companion in the blanket.

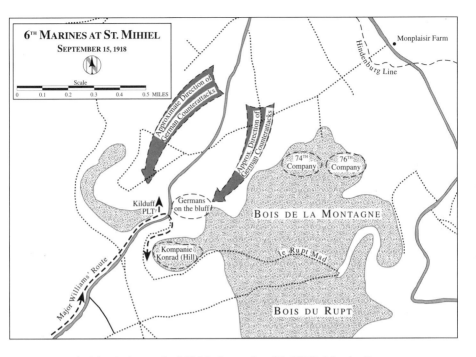

Map 5. 6th Marines at St. Mihiel, September 15, 1918. Map by Peter F. Owen.

In the meantime, the battalion deployed back of us, and, falling back with it, we made preparations to try and hold our position against an assault. I was in the woods, facing the open ground where our platoon had suffered such heavy casualties. They first shelled us and then assaulted, but we held our ground. During the shelling, we lay flat on our stomachs. As soon as it stopped, a fellow named Hines who was lying beside me didn't come up very fast to grab his rifle.[15] I pulled down his shirt with one hand, handling my rifle with the other, and found a slug of the shrapnel buried in his shoulder. He pulled himself together, however, and fought like an able-bodied man.

The Americans on each flank fought up even with us, and we were out of an embarrassing situation. We were relieved by the 78th Division for their first time on the front lines.[16] As we were walking away from the front at St. Mihiel and out of shell fire, some ladies served cookies and a cup of chocolate to each one of us. One of the ladies was Mrs. Astor of New York.[17]

Chapter 5

Blanc
Mont

Before the offensive at St. Mihiel had even commenced,
Pershing's staff had plunged headlong into plans for an
American offensive in the Meuse-Argonne. The terrible
battles of the spring and summer had bled the German
Army at a rate beyond its capacity to provide replacements, while fresh American troops poured off ships onto
French docks. Generalissimo Ferdinand Foch smelled victory: he ordered offensives across the Western Front.
The American attack in the Argonne would begin on September 26, a scant ten days after the 2nd Division had
been relieved in the St. Mihiel sector.[1]

In order to bolster the battered French Army, Pershing
offered Pétain the use of the U.S. 2nd and 36th Divisions. As the Franco-American offensive commenced on
September 26, these two formations were in the general reserve of the French Army. There was little doubt
that the American 2nd Division would move up to a tight
spot soon, once again under French command.

On September 27, General Lejeune heard a rumor that
his 2nd Division would be divided among separate French
Corps. He demanded and received an immediate interview with General Gouraud, the commander of the Fourth
French Army. Gouraud explained that, while the
doughboys of the First American Army had struggled to

make progress in the Argonne, his own army had stalled a scant dozen miles to the west in front of a series of high areas known as "Les Monts." The key to the German defense hinged on Blanc Mont; if it fell into French hands, the Germans would have no choice but to fall back on the next natural defensive barrier thirty kilometers to the north. The capture of Blanc Mont would rejuvenate the French offensive and relieve pressure on the Americans in the Argonne.

Lejeune sensed an opportunity to guarantee that his division would not be divided and promptly volunteered his boys for this most difficult assignment. In his memoirs, he wrote: "I answered with deliberation, 'General, if you do not divide the Second Division, but put it in line as a unit on a narrow front, I am confident that it will be able to take Blanc Mont Ridge, advance beyond it, and hold its position there.'"[2]

Blanc Mont is roughly an L-shaped ridge. The long axis of the L runs east-west, while the base of the L points southward, toward the Allied lines. The slope begins just north of the village of Sommepy and rises gently to the north for three kilometers (almost two miles) to a height of two hundred feet at the summit. The ground is open grassland, dotted with occasional scrub pine. It offers excellent fields of fire.

The German 1st Defensive Line consisted of four trenches at the base of the slope in front of Sommepy. The 2nd Defensive Line ran along the crest of the long axis of the L, two kilometers to the north. In between the two positions lay the outpost zone of the 2nd Line, a network of machine-gun emplacements similar to the positions the 80th Company had run into at St. Mihiel.

The 80th Company and the 2nd Battalion filtered into a captured section of the 1st Line during the night of October 1–2. In preparation for the division's attack, planned for the morning of October 3, the 2nd Battalion went "over the top" on the evening of October 2 to clear the Germans from the last of the 1st Line trenches. Luck was with the marines, for the Germans had abandoned these positions, and the battalion suffered only a few wounded.[3]

At St. Mihiel, the 2nd Battalion had followed the rest of the division into the attack. This time, Major Williams' marines formed the first wave, with the remainder of the 4th Brigade stacked up behind them. Williams set his companies from left to right in the following order: 96th, 78th, 80th, and 79th. Off to the right somewhere lay the doughboys of the 3rd Brigade, who would link up with the marines on the summit of Blanc Mont. To the left lay *poilus* of the French 21st Division.[4]

These *poilus* on the marines' left faced a commanding east-west ridge directly to their front. The Germans had not evacuated the 1st Line trenches running along this ridge. This created a peculiar situation in which the marines occupied the same line of trenches as the Germans, with an unoccupied section between Brannen's battalion and the Germans on the ridge.

The fourth of these German trenches, called the Essen Trench, ran along the north side of the ridge, where it was invulnerable to fire from the south. The Americans dubbed this position the "Essen Hook." If the French could not take this ridge and keep up with the Americans, the German machine gunners could pour a withering fire into the marine ranks from the left rear. Col. Harry Lee, commander of the 6th Marines, requested that the position be neutralized by artillery fire if it could not be captured.[5]

The attack began at 5:55 A.M., after a surprise five-minute barrage. The 2nd Battalion advanced up the slope behind a rolling barrage, moving one hundred meters every four minutes to keep with the pace. The battalion's left sector limit would brush the base of the L as the marines climbed toward their objective, the summit of Blanc Mont.[6]

We now got replacements to take the place of our killed and wounded and drilled while wondering where the next call would be. Within ten days after leaving the lines, the Americans began the Argonne battle, one of the most stubborn and bloody ever fought by them. We were swinging a door by pushing near the hinges. A small gain in the Argonne Forest caused a longer gain up toward Flanders.

Further up from the forest near Rheims, the French were meeting with poor success. My division was sent to their assistance. We were loaded on trucks and rushed to the front before Blanc Mont Ridge, passing through the city of Chalons late the evening of October 1st.

Horace Cooper, who was wounded at the battle of Soissons, had recovered and returned, and we became buddies. Scatterbrain was either killed or was wounded again, so it was some consolation to fall in with one I had been associated with before.[7] The buddy system worked well because of the companionship, and at night behind the lines one could lay his blanket on the ground for both and cover with the other, as each man carried only one blanket.

The orders to attack were delayed twenty-four hours and we spent all day of the 2nd looking ahead at the long high chalky ridge honeycombed with dugouts. The French had tried to carry this position several times and failed. Their dead were sprawled around in the trench as grim reminders of the fighting that had been going on here for several days.

The St. Mihiel ambush and the Soissons experience, when I was alone and among the enemy, made twice that my platoon had been annihilated and I had survived. Lieutenants Overton and Kilduff had been killed. I knew that my time would come sooner or later. The Marine song had the words in it, "If the Army and the Navy ever look on Heaven's scenes/They will find the streets are guarded by the United States Marines." After looking at that ridge ahead, I decided that my next duty might be helping guard the heavenly streets. As it turned out, that was almost the case.

Two or three hours before daylight, the word was passed along to get ready for the attack. Everyone checked his bayonet to see that it was fastened on good with the latch. Ammunition was inspected, and the flaps of the belt unhooked so that a fresh clip could be gotten into the rifle quickly. Each man had two extra bandoleers of ammunition around his shoulders. I made sure the bandoleers of ammunition were in front of my chest. The issued razor was in the right-hand pocket of my blouse and the YMCA-issued Bible was in the left-hand pocket. I was using all of the protection that I could think of.

Just as it was breaking day (zero hour), we came out of our trench and began the ascent in combat formation. The rows of men moved forward unhesitatingly but fell like ten pins before the deadly machine-gun fire. I was a runner to carry messages from flank to flank of my company and the one adjoining, trying to keep the units in contact with each other as the now thin lines swept over the crest.

I was with a lieutenant of the 78th company when we entered the forest of small pines which were along the crest and down its slopes on the other side. We were firing on the retreating enemy as we advanced, sometimes dropping to a knee for better aim. A bullet hit my bayonet about an inch from the muzzle of the rifle while I was carrying it at Port Arms position, shattering the bayonet and leaving me only a stub. A Marine near me rushed at three Germans who were also near. I speeded up and rushed at them, too, with my rifle lowered to use my bayonet. They surrendered, and then I noticed them looking at my bayonet. I tried to read their minds. They must have thought that I had broken off my bayonet in a man. Later a man in my company saw me with my stub of a bayonet and said, "Old Brannen stuck his bayonet in one and broke it off."

While passing a dead German officer, I noticed a pair of field glasses around his neck and, knowing their skill in making this article, I stooped down and took them off him, placing the strap around my own neck. Passing a deep dugout which we figured held some of the enemy, we hollered down to come out but got no answer. We then dropped in a couple of hand grenades, and about twenty came out at another entrance several feet away with hands over their heads in token of surrender.

A machine-gun nest was now holding up the advance. Instead of trying a direct assault, we decided to flank it. The lieutenant asked for some men to go around each flank. Three of us went to the left. When we were in close proximity to the nest, we were a little too exposed, and the fellow on my right fell, killed. As I jumped for protection into a ditch nearby, a fusillade of bullets caught me below the heart on the left side, through one lens of the field glasses, and against my bandoleer of ammunition. The best I remember, ten bullets in my own belt exploded, but they had deflected the enemy bullets, saving my life. My own bullets ripped my coat to shreds as they exploded and went out over my left shoulder by the side of my face. My cloth bandoleer and the field glasses caught on fire. I got them off me and then replaced the field glasses around my neck again as they quit burning.

I collected myself together and, with the other companion in the ditch, looked for our machine gunner but saw that Americans were now in possession. I suppose we had helped by drawing fire while the others rushed, for on going up there I found three dead Germans stretched [out] by two guns. One must have gotten away, as it took two for each gun. Machine gun-

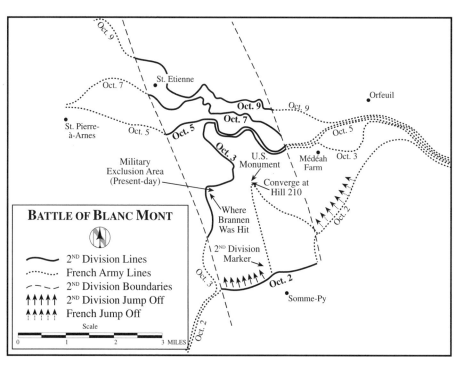

Map 6. Blanc Mont, October 3, 1918. Map by J. P. Brannen.

ners were never taken prisoners by either side. A machine gunner's only chance was to be taken while he was away from the gun and his captors did not know he had any connection with it. The reason is obvious, for when a man sat behind a gun and mowed down a bunch of men, his life was automatically forfeited.

We stopped and began forming a line along a road. Just ahead, three Germans showed themselves in a trench. Sherwood and I dashed over, and they came out surrendering.[8] They were shaking like a leaf and saying "Telephonique." They were telling us that they worked on keeping up the telephone lines to the front and had no connection with the machine-gun nest which gave me such a raking over and had just been captured.

I had bled over my coat from a bullet striking a brad in the rifle sling and ricocheting the brad into my upper lip. I also thought the scratches in my side should be iodined. The prisoners afforded an excuse for leaving the lines, so I started back with them. As I passed some of my company, they stretched their eyes at the number of bullet holes in my clothes while I grinned at them.

As I got away from any other American soldiers, the prisoners began to stretch out and make too much space between them, so I just prodded the back one with the stub of my bayonet and made him keep up. Back a little ways, I ran into a French officer who in broken English asked me to bring my prisoners to help him with some wounded. They seemed to resent this Frenchman more than they did me, but I made them go and went with them. Shells had almost wiped out a battery of artillery, and the bodies of the men were terribly mangled. We helped bring two of the wounded away.[9] Continuing, I ran into some MPs and turned over my prisoners. Returning toward the line, I went by a first-aid station which had been hurriedly thrown up beside the road, expecting to get painted with iodine. The doctor who was a major looked me over, asked me how long I had been with the outfit, and then to my surprise tagged me for the hospital.[10] An ambulance carried a bunch of us back to a field hospital that night. A group of Americans back there when we unloaded from the ambulance ganged around and asked a thousand questions. They marveled at my miraculous escape.[11]

I was placed on my back on a table in a little room with a doctor on each side. They placed some kind of machine over my wound and were looking through it apparently. They seemed to have discovered a bullet inside of me when one of them found that they were looking at a button on the back of my pants. I felt quite relieved when the examination showed that no bullets had penetrated, but had only ragged the flesh a little. A German prisoner was near me with his right arm almost shattered in two at the elbow.

I was so inexperienced at sleeping off the ground and on springs that sleep did not come as readily as I expected. A day here and I was placed on a hospital train with many more to go to Base Hospital #27 at Angers, across France near Bordeaux. I unloaded at night, discarded the muddy, bloody clothes, took a good bath, put on clean pajamas, and crawled between two clean white sheets.

My ward was filled with men with all kinds of wounds. In the morning a nurse came along and took temperatures, which judged what a fellow would get to eat. Next came the doctor and "agony wagon" and so through the days until you were pronounced fit to leave.

Day after day the doctors skillfully worked at their trade, amputating, patching, and snatching men from the grave. In spite of all this, there was a funeral every few days. They would not issue clothes until you left. So, after catching up on my rest, I began slipping out and going to town, walking around in pajamas and house shoes.

From here I was sent with several others to Le Mon, where we received equipment and headed back for the front. We were routed to where our division would be and reached there ahead of time. While strolling around the little village near the Argonne Forest and wondering where my outfit was, I noticed a cloud of dust in the distance and upon closer observation made out a line of trucks approaching one behind the other. I stood on the sidewalk and watched the old reliable 2nd Division of Regulars and Marines roll through and unload two miles out. As these grim-visaged veterans of Belleau Wood, Soissons, Pont-a-Mousson, St. Mihiel, and Mont Blanc passed through, I heard those there in the town remark, "All hell is going to break loose up front. Those blankety-blank Marines are going up."

I walked on the two miles to where they unloaded and gave Cooper an extra pair of clean underwear which I had brought along. Was he glad to get them and discard those cootie nests he was wearing.

Chapter 6

The Meuse-Argonne

The railroad had contributed as much to the stalemate on the Western Front as had the machine gun and barbed wire. Machine guns could create a temporary deadlock, but it took trains—hundreds of trains a day—to supply the millions of men, millions of rounds, and millions of tons of supplies needed to sustain an army in uninterrupted combat. The German Army on the Western Front depended upon two main railways for its supply lifeline. One of these railroads ran through Sedan, about thirty-five kilometers to the north of where the Hindenburg Line cut through the Argonne. By cutting this railroad, or just by clawing his way close enough to hit it with long-range artillery, Pershing hoped to achieve a colossal interruption in German logistics.

While the 2nd Division had fought for Blanc Mont, the American First Army had struggled bitterly since September 26 for indecisive gains in the Argonne. Pershing ambitiously had hoped to break the Hindenburg Line, ten miles to the German rear, on the first day. But at least forty-eight hours before the attack, the German Fifth Army commander, General von Gallwitz, had deduced the location where the main First Army attack would fall. He had ordered up reinforcements in time to stop the doughboys in their tracks. While the British and French offensives gained momentum, a second U.S. attack on

October 4 had to be followed up with a third on October 14 before the Hindenburg Line was within reach. (The Hindenburg Line had been breached on the American right where it curved to the southeast, but in most sectors it remained just beyond the front-line American troops.) Faced with its first tough assignment, the American army had bogged down far short of the rail line through Sedan.[1]

The First Army covered a front sixteen miles wide, from the Argonne Forest in the west to the Meuse River in the east. Its path ran smack into the toughest ground on the Western Front. Steep, open ridges with wonderful fields of fire—miniature Blanc Monts—covered most of the sector. High ground east of the Meuse allowed German artillery spotters to direct fire with impunity throughout most of the American sector. The few muddy farm roads caused considerable traffic delays—delays which left infantry without ammunition, without food, and without artillery support.

Pershing planned his fourth attack for November 1. Three corps, with seven divisions, lined up across the front. The 2nd Division, as part of the V Corps in the center, was tasked to seize a series of ridges called Barricourt Heights four miles beyond the Hindenburg Line. Lejeune planned to attack with the Marine brigade for the first phase of the attack, then pass the doughboys of the 3rd Brigade through after the marines had taken Barricourt Heights. As the main effort of the entire offensive, the 2nd Division had been reinforced with all of the machine guns and artillery of the 42nd Division, as well as with the only fifteen tanks which the American army could muster. The marines were told to take Barricourt Heights the first day.[2]

Lejeune's soldiers and marines outnumbered the enemy in the division sector by a ratio of roughly two to one. German infantry strength numbered something around forty-eight hundred troops. Two artillery regiments and a separate artillery battalion were emplaced in the draws behind each ridge the marines would cross. Additional German divisions were expected to counterattack after the first few hours.[3]

General Neville, commanding the Marine brigade, placed the 5th Marines on the right and the 6th Marines on the left. In the 6th Marine Regiment, the 1st Battalion would go over the top initially, followed by the 3rd Battalion in support and Brannen's 2nd Battalion in reserve. After the 1st Battalion had seized the Hindenburg Line position just south of Landres–St. George, the other battalions would pass through the 1st, with the 3rd Battalion leading through

Bayonville. North of Bayonville, the 2nd Battalion would pass through the 3rd and assault Barricourt Heights.[4]

Just prior to the previous American attacks in this sector, German machine gunners had crawled as far forward as possible in order to slip inside the American barrage. In the 2nd Division sector, the marines pulled back their front line about three hundred yards shortly before the scheduled barrage. The barrage would now catch the German machine gunners by surprise, falling on top of the vacated American positions.

At 3:30 A.M., the greatest American barrage of the war shattered the cold, misty night. Artillery pieces packed to a density of one cannon for every ten yards of front rained shells on the German troops huddled in their dugouts.[5] Over 250 machine guns poured millions of rounds into the German positions.[6]

After two hours, the shelling culminated with a ten-minute standing barrage on top of the vacated front line. This ten-minute barrage allowed the 1st Battalion to close up and "lean into" the shells. At 5:40, the marines stepped off, pacing closely behind the shrapnel clouds, which moved a hundred yards every four minutes. As at Blanc Mont, the marines were on top of the battered defenders before they could collect their wits.[7]

We took up the march to the front over wet boggy roads, but stopped on one of the hills in this war-devastated region while things were gotten in readiness for a new attack. It didn't seem necessary any more to try and launch a surprise attack. While we were waiting here, General Summerall, who was commanding our army corps, went from group to group of our division, getting on a stump where the Germans had been logging the forest and speaking to us about like this: "It is now the last of October and way past time when the army should dig in for the winter and wait until spring for active operations again. You men have compiled an enviable record. We could stop and wait for spring, but I believe by pushing on we can end it this year." I didn't put much faith in the ending part, but an American always stands ready to do [the country's] bidding, as conveyed through her high officer.

We took over the line October 31 and the next morning, after the artillery preparation, went over the top behind our barrage. The fighting was fierce until we took their trench. The nozzle of a ten-inch shell hit me a glancing blow in the chest, but the folds of my overcoat helped, and I had a narrow escape. We fought on across a cemetery, and while crossing it I noticed that the tombstones were all shattered and chipped from machine-gun bullets, rifle bullets, and shrapnel.

Sometime in the afternoon we lost Captain Green, who was now commanding, and all of the lieutenants. The top sergeant was commanding the remnant of the company.[8] By late evening of the first day of this battle it was raining, and it kept up continuously, except when it was too cold. We were drenched to the skin, and it was freezing. At night we lay in the mud, tired and hungry, and in the morning would take up the advance again.[9]

The men were nearly all affected with dysentery from the scanty unfit food and polluted water. Before drinking from wells, which were nearly all poisoned, we would wait until a doctor made an examination and in order to counteract the poison he would add another poison which purified the water but left it with a taste about like the worst medicine. We were all weak and exhausted.[10] This kept up for ten days until we reached the Meuse River. The city of Sedan, where Napoleon III was captured in 1871, was occupied while my particular outfit had captured the little city of Beaumont. The river was high from the incessant raining, but the night of the 10th of November we got orders to cross.[11] While the pontoon bridge was being made ready in pitch darkness, some of us went over where a big ammunition dump was burning and tried to thaw out. When retreating, the idea is to burn or destroy everything you can't carry. We found big fine horses shot down because they could not be moved.

The boats were tied side by side and a plank laid across them to walk on. When this bridge was made long enough to reach across the stream, the lower end was tied to our side and a soldier took the other end, swimming the cold treacherous river, and fastened it to the other side. The troops carried their equipment, ammunition, and rifles in their hands so as to have a better chance to get out if they made a wrong step in the darkness. In the morning we had a foothold on the opposite bank.[12]

A few days before we had heard rumors of peace, plenipotentiaries having come through the lines further up north, but [we] considered it only another false report. A few weeks be-

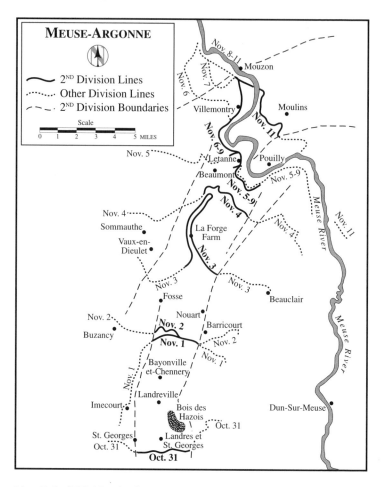

Map 7. 2nd Division in the Meuse-Argonne, Oct. 25–Nov. 11, 1918.
Map by Peter F. Owen.

fore we had heard that German troops had mutinied and killed the Kaiser.

At 11 o'clock [on] November 11 we were told that an armistice was in effect and were ordered not to fire another shot. These orders were very easily obeyed. That night you could see fires up and down the front where the men were warming and sleeping. This would have been unthinkable before.[13]

After a few hours' sleep, I tried to look around for something to eat. We spent about a week trying to clean ourselves up, being reinforced, equipped, and exploring around. It was marvelous to see our kitchen right out in the open, the artillery

View across the Meuse at Mouzon bridge, 1918. Photo No. 127-G-35YY-519376, National Archives, Washington, D.C.

horses grazing out in the open, and to walk around without being afraid of someone taking a potshot at you.

About the 17th we took up the march, passing out of France across southern Belgium and across Luxembourg to the border of Germany, where we stopped. This took a week or more of steady hiking. Our advance guard kept contact with the German rear guard. While they would be leaving a village on one side, we were entering on the other. The inhabitants, who had been in occupied territory for over four years, were overcome with joy. They met us before we got in the village waving homemade American flags. They were not accurate on the number of stars or stripes, but we knew their intentions were right. Usually some of the feminine sex would break into ranks and shower a kiss or so on a lucky fellow.

I had received a letter from home after the battle of Soissons, and it was all for the seven months I had been in France. However, at this time I got a carload. It took me a day or two of reading, when I could, to read them all. I had not drawn any pay for the same length of time. I got paid up all of my back pay in French money, which amounted to about fourteen hundred francs.

Sergeant O'Kelley had disappeared in the Belleau Wood fighting, and we figured that he was killed, but about this time he came in from a German prison camp. His platoon had attacked a strong German position by rushing it. By the time the sergeant got within a few feet of the spouting machine guns, all of his men were down, including himself. A bullet had wounded his scalp, but it only dazed him. However, when he fell, a dead man fell across him, and he lay there the rest of the day. After dark he began trying to wiggle from under his burden, but it was light enough for the enemy to see the movement, and they came out and got him. I sure was glad to see him and hear of his experience as a prisoner.[14]

Army
of
Occupation

Chapter 7

The armistice had brought neither peace nor an end to the trials of the 2nd Division, but a cessation of hostilities and an introduction to miseries of a different order. The division remained on a war footing throughout its march to the Rhineland and for much of the occupation. The march to Germany proved to be one of the most difficult of the war. The horrible conditions in the Meuse-Argonne had weakened even the fittest marines. An average march of twenty to thirty kilometers lasted seven tedious hours; one march of forty-two kilometers was an ordeal. Inferior British boots issued just prior to the march caused so many foot injuries that some men preferred to march in their socks.[1]

The 80th Company reached its new home at Rhein-brohl, near Koblenz, in mid-December. In an effort to maintain the AEF's fighting edge, Pershing embarked on a rigorous postwar training plan to keep the soldiers ready for another outbreak in hostilities, as well as to keep the boys busy. The 2nd Division posted its sentries and trained through the winter. Morale plummeted in some other units, as the soldiers felt little inclination to train for a war they had already won, in an army they were now eager to leave.[2]

Training eventually gave way to athletics and other diversions. One hazard not encountered by Private

Brannen, but an interesting footnote to the occupation, was an outbreak of venereal disease. A liberal leave policy resulted in an increase of venereal disease among marines who visited France, but reports of venereal disease contracted from German women remained infrequent. "For a while it was thought the anti-fraternization orders were responsible for the low rate of venereal infection traceable to source in Germany." But the surgeons soon determined that the marines feared a court-martial more than they feared the consequences of foregoing treatment. "Those applying for prophylaxis had been required to complete a venereal disease form, on which the name and address of the 'woman in the case' had to be given." This form could then be used as evidence against marines on a charge of fraternization. The 6th Marines surgeon took steps to change this policy. It soon developed that most cases involved "for the most part country women with whom there were wide-scale relations."[3]

Between training, sentry duty, inspections, leave, and sports, the marines whiled away what, for many, was the first exposure to "routine" life in the Marine Corps. It compared dully with life at the front, but it was, on the whole, comfortable and decidedly less dangerous than combat. But the question foremost in every marine's mind was: "When do we go home?"

We stayed in Luxembourg several days before going into Germany, and spent the time patrolling the little river at the border. By this time we had gotten some new clothes, and the cooties were a thing of the past. We also got some new equipment, and I was issued a new Browning machine gun. How I would liked to have had it while I was back on the front instead of that French Chau Chau. It seemed that we were to try and make as good and as formidable an appearance as possible when the German people got their first look at an invading army of occupation.[4]

On the first day of December, we were up early and on the march by daylight. As our column of troops crossed the boundary, the men and women seemed to ignore our passing as if nothing out of the ordinary was happening. I know the men were our late adversaries, even though they were standing around in civilian clothes. It was different with the children. They stared at us in wide-eyed wonder.

The schedule was to march fifty minutes and rest ten out of each hour. The officers evidently had gotten strict orders from higher up, for they were exacting and very alert, as if we were on the front and might be attacked at any time. There were to be two meals a day, morning and night, and no one could drink water except from his canteen, without permission. This was a precaution against drinking poison water.

My machine gun with the ammunition [for it] was about twice as heavy as a rifle and its ammunition, giving me a disadvantage with most of the other soldiers. In the evening we began to look forward to stopping and getting off our weary legs. A little after dark we passed through a pretty good-sized town and, so sure of having reached our destination were we, that singing began, but [it] died out as we went through without stopping. By this time the ten-minute rest had been abandoned, for we could not have risen with our packs once we got down.

Men were soon falling down by the roadside, exhausted. Major Metcalf threatened, but when a fellow had done all he could, that could avail nothing.[5] I don't know how it was done, but I was still trudging along and able to crawl over on a pile of hay in a barn about ten o'clock that night when we bivouacked. The day's objective had been reached. We had made forty kilometers walking that day.

I had walked until I was completely exhausted many times before, but I believe this one remained in my memory the best. About twelve o'clock that night, the kitchens caught up and announced chow, but I could not get up to go after the slum gullion and did without supper. The next morning we were up and on the march by daylight, after eating breakfast. I had some difficulty in getting my legs to moving again.

Our route in Germany was down the valley of the Ahr River, which we had to follow because the mountains on either side could not have been crossed. So winding was the river that we traveled three or four times what the distance would have been in a straight line. The scenery was wonderful, if only I could have enjoyed the walking a little more.

By the 12th of December we reached the Rhine River, after going around three hundred miles on foot.[6] That night we put out guards as usual, but this time Cooper and I were the "Watch on the Rhine." The two of us walked our post up and down the river bank some few paces apart. This precaution was so that if someone tried to shoot the sentinels, he might not get both.

[On] the 13th, a squad of eight of us crossed the river in a motor boat and scattered out in the little town of Honnigen to guard the crossing of the regiment. About twenty little Dutch boys from eight to twelve years of age, who evidently were on their way to school, gathered around me and jabbered as I stood sentinel at a street intersection. I was the first invading soldier they had ever viewed. They pointed out my equipment to each other, talking all the time. One pointed at my machine gun and said "Boom! Boom!" Another unrolled his sandwich of brown bread with butter and marmalade between and offered it to me.

After crossing, we went up the river toward Coblenz three or four miles to Rheinbrohl, where I remained almost six months in the "Army of Occupation." During the winter we went up in the hills and dug trenches and practiced shooting. If the Germans refused to sign the peace treaty, we had a good jumping off place toward Berlin.

When the Armistice was signed, the American troops who had just arrived overseas loaded back on the boats for the return, then the next closest to the ports of embarkation, and so on. In other words, the troop movement was reversed. We on the front lines thought this unfair, but orders were orders, and it was more economical this way.

General Black Jack concentrated the different divisions of the army of occupation and inspected each one. Our division was inspected near Coblenz, where the Kaiser had inspected his army corps before they left for the Western Front. When our twenty-eight thousand men assembled, it must have been near half a mile from one flank to the other. It was estimated that the general walked about ten miles in going through the ranks. He then called the noncommissioned officers together and complimented them on the division's record in the war. The thing he said that sounded best was the fact that we would soon return to the good old U.S.A.

General Pershing's Honor Guard

Chapter 8

After several months in the Army of Occupation, Private Brannen joined the ranks of the American Expeditionary Forces Composite Regiment, commonly referred to as "Pershing's Own." It was no small distinction to be chosen for this select group, and Brannen justifiably felt proud. As the showpiece of the American army, the regiment needed men of imposing stature and impeccable bearing—giant, spit-shined, parade-ground soldiers. Joining the regiment afforded doughboys a break from occupation duties and gave them a whirlwind tour of France and England. In Brannen's case the battalion commander selected men who had distinguished themselves in combat, which was no mean feat in that unit. As Brannen, by his own admission, was one of the shortest men in this honor guard, presumably he had distinguished himself a good deal more than he let on in his memoir.

Carl Brannen had distinguished himself as a member of another select group, to be sure. He had fought with the 4th Marine Brigade in every major battle, seeing its ranks thinned and replenished many times. When it was all over, he walked down the gangplank onto a pier in New York City, alive and well.

Pitifully few could claim as much.

General Pershing now ordered a regiment for parading purposes to be formed from the Army of Occupation, which called for selecting about one man out of each thirty. In my division, men were selected who had had lots of front line service, and my joy knew no bounds when I was selected by Major Barker and his committee.[1]

Before leaving our old Sixth Regiment, Colonel Harry Lee, who I have been told was a relative of the celebrated Lees of Virginia, called us together and gave some parting advice. We were representing America before Europe. I'm sure Robert E. Lee's men could not have loved him much more than I did Colonel Harry. He is dead now, but I will always carry a mental picture of him as he was during our fighting in Belleau Wood.[2]

We were concentrated at Coblenz for a month's intensive training, and I really put out to keep from falling down and being sent back to my outfit. This was a group of real veterans. Most of them had been wounded on the front, and a large majority were wearing decorations for some outstanding feat of bravery. The band to accompany the regiment was chosen after some days of contesting by several bands.

In June we went by rail back to General Pershing's headquarters in Paris. We crossed the old front line at Verdun, and while the train ran slowly I looked out across "Dead Man's Hill," where thousands of wooden crosses dotted the hillside and thought of how near I came to being under one.

Our barracks were in the Bois de Vincennes, about two hundred yards from a trolley line. We could ride the trolley a short way to the first subway station, and from there we could be rapidly transferred to any place in the city. I now put all of my back pay into circulation. It was the sights of Paris instead of the scenery up and down the Rhine River.

On July 4, we participated in a parade through the city and wound up with the laying of a wreath on Lafayette's grave. On July 14, Bastille Day, a parade the like of which may never be equaled was held in Paris. Days ahead of time, bleachers were erected along the Champs Elysees Boulevard for the notables and the crowd. As I walked along the boulevard before the parade, I met an American woman who was the consul's wife and got lots of information about Paris from her.

The French threw themselves into preparing for the triumphant march. The great Arc of Triumph, constructed by Napo-

Composite regiment on parade in Paris, 1919. Photo No. SC-14965
DD-MC-529659, National Archives, Washington, D.C.

leon, had huge chains on concrete posts set in the ground around
it so that the German soldiers couldn't march under it in 1871,
when they captured Paris. The chain was now opened so that
France and her allies could march under the Arc. The day of
the parade the population of the city was estimated at ten mil-
lion. Marshal Foch led, followed by General Pershing and staff
on prancing steeds and the crack American regiment. Then came
a representation of every Allied force, including the Arabians
on their camels and the picturesque kilted Scots.

A few days later, the general carried us with him by rail to
Le Havre, across the English Channel by boat to Southamp-
ton, then by rail to London, where a similar parade was held
July 19, on Empire Day. That parade was exactly a year from
the day that I lay in the old road under the German machine
gun and got with Lieutenant Cates later in the evening. Cates
was now a captain and commander of my company in the honor
guard regiment.

King George with the royal family and high officials of England were in the receiving stand to receive our salute as we passed. During the two weeks stay in London, our regiment was given a personal inspection by the Prince of Wales (later Edward VIII) in Hyde Park. I also visited Buckingham Palace, Kensington Palace, Westminster Abbey, the House of Parliament, the Tower of London, Charles Dickens' home, and General Haig's home.

The British colonial troops were being cleared through England and sent home as rapidly as possible. Our regiment was quartered near some Australian troops. There were those among them who had left home as mere boys but were now full-fledged veterans and had not seen their homeland in over four years. The expense of allowing men to have a leave of absence for such a long ways was not to be thought of.

Despite the fact that the battle over who won the war was raging in full fury at this time, we had a very enjoyable time in England. Slurs were hurled at us, such as "You Yanks think you won the war. Where were you in 1914?" However, their committee of hospitality to the Americans, with John Burns of the House of Commons as an outstanding figure, really functioned. According to history, Burns of the Labor Party was similar to our Theodore Roosevelt.

One night at a theater party given for us, the general told the British in a little speech that they were killing us with kindness. After our parades, the *London Daily Mail* gave the Americans quite a writeup and compared us favorably with their Coldstream Guards, which was quite a compliment.

Men of our regiment of honor guard for the general were picked from a physical standpoint. I was one of the smallest men in it, standing five feet, eight and one-half inches and weighing one hundred sixty pounds at this time.

The return to Paris was made by the same route, [and] there we remained until near the latter part of August. An American guard remained on duty with the stars and stripes at the Hôtel de Ville, which was occupied by President Wilson during the peace conference. The day the German delegates filed into Versailles Palace and signed, officially closing the war, Paris went into a frenzy. Traffic was completely tied up while the celebration lasted all day and night.

Captain Cates was very lenient with us but required strict obedience and a good appearance at all times and, above all, no bobbles in parading before the public. We could come and go almost at will. We were supplied with good clothes, equipment, plenty to eat, and lots of privileges, but we were to be in camp at certain times each day. I got tied up in the big celebration in the city and was gone the day and night. I was expecting to get in bad with the captain, but I found that there were many more in my predicament, and I suspect the captain himself celebrated with them.

A great concrete stadium was built by the Americans in Paris and dedicated Pershing Stadium. Here were held the Inter-Allied Games, participated in by athletes from all the Allied countries. I am sure it was very much like the Olympics. Our regiment paraded on the opening day, passing in review before the giants of that day, such as Poincairé, Clemenceau, and others. We also gave an exhibition drill. At one time during the parade, a slight mistake was made in halting, due to lack of room. This was the only one I ever noted during my five months in this organization.

Some of the outstanding athletes who participated for America were Charles Paddock, LeGendre, Joie Ray, the Negro sprint star De Hart Hubbard, and Gene Tunney. I thought of Johnny Overton, my lieutenant who was killed at Soissons, and thought of how he would have strutted in some of the races.

Finally orders came to leave Paris. While we were leaving, I noticed a wistful look in some soldiers' eyes as the mademoiselles present hummed "Apre la guerre finis American Parte."

At Brest, every man was thoroughly inspected for diseases, and I was pulled out of ranks with the scabies, or just common itch. Several of us were put in a quarantine camp, made to smear ourselves from head to foot with sulphur and grease, and wear a suit of dungarees for three days without changing. I was beginning to get uneasy for fear the outfit would move on and leave me. We were pronounced pure again, and I hurried back to the barracks.

While I was some distance off, I could hear joyous singing and see lots of bustling around. I walked up on the company packing up to go aboard ship for the good old U.S.A. and home. I fell to with a will and soon had a neat pack that would have made old Sergeant Boynton back in Parris Island days smile. Some of the gang were returning after an absence of twenty-seven months. I had been gone eighteen, and that seemed too long.

We went aboard the *Leviathan,* the largest ship afloat at that time, and what a contrast with the *Henderson*! It was so large that it could not dock in the Brest Harbor but stood out at sea while we went out in smaller boats. In time everyone was aboard, including General Black Jack, and what a difference from the trip over. There was plenty of room, the ship didn't rock so much, and we crossed in less than half the previous time.

The morning of September 8, our ship steamed past the Statue of Liberty in New York Harbor and docked. While we were coming in, seventeen guns were fired as a salute to the full-fledged general aboard. America had produced only a few full generals. Washington was the first, followed by Grant, Sherman, and Pershing. The harbor was full of welcoming craft, including the major's boat. Evidently a prearranged schedule was followed, for suddenly every ship whistle and every factory whistle in New York opened up at the same time, and what a deafening sound.

We went to Camp Mills on Long Island, from which place we went by rail to the heart of the city and formed lines. About ten o'clock the parade began down Fifth Avenue, proceeding through Wall Street and the important parts of the city. Pershing and his staff led, followed by our regiment and then the entire 1st Division. This parade was as long [as], or longer than, those in London and Paris. It ended by twelve o'clock with us still in the heart of the city, after having marched ten miles without stopping. The honor guards were then served a sumptuous plate lunch.

From here we went to Washington, D.C., where a similar parade was held September 17, down historic Pennsylvania Avenue. This was the first time a fully equipped army had paraded through Washington since the Civil War, when the conquering army returned from the South.

There was some talk about keeping the honor guard regiment together and parading through the large cities of the nation, but this was abandoned as expensive and maybe because of politics. The 1920 presidential campaign was coming on, and it might seem that Pershing was being pushed as a Republican nominee.[3] The regiment was broken up, and we marines were sent to the marine barracks in Washington, D.C.

I had now been in the service almost two years, during which time I had never been any closer [to my] home in Texas than South Carolina. I had changed from an eighteen-year-old boy without any beard into a twenty-year-old veteran with a full set of whiskers. I had enlisted for four years but was allowed to transfer into the reserve, subject to call, and drawing pay of a dollar a month.

I stopped in New Orleans on the way home and bought a forty-seven-dollar suit of clothes with part of my sixty-dollar bonus. By the time I completed my wardrobe, [the money] was gone.

Soon after reaching home, I started working for a company, but I was told I would have to get a minor's release from my father, since my twenty-first birthday had not been reached.

At the end of the four years, I received my discharge. The War Department, after checking and rechecking, has released the following figures on casualties for my regiment. The 6th Regiment, composed of 3,000 men, had 1,161 killed in action or died of wounds, and 4,656 wounded, for total casualties of 5,817 (*The Indian Head*, Jan. 1929). It was wiped out and replaced almost twice. The 2nd Battalion was composed of the 78th, 79th, 80th, and 96th companies. This battalion had two boys in it from Trinity County, Texas. Roy Trow of the 79th Company was killed in the battle of Belleau Wood [on] June 7.[4] I was in the 80th Company; I was commanded by General Smedley (Blanco) Butler for a while, but my brigade on the front was commanded by General Neville.[5]

C. A. Brannen's Scrapbook

Pvt. C. A. Brannen, USMC, during
Army of Occupation era, 1919.

Horace Cooper rests his hand on C. A. Brannen's shoulder in this
photo taken in postwar Germany, 1919. The marine to their left is
armed with a BAR and a .45 pistol.

Pvt. Horace J. Cooper arrived in Brannen's group of replacements to join the 80th Company on June 8. He was wounded in the arm and leg and part of his ear at Soissons.

Four marines of the 80th Company, February 1919. *Clockwise from left:* Pvt. John D. Chestnut; unknown; Pvt. Charles Fanning; Pvt. Ole Gunderson. Uniforms and insignia were more casual in the World War I than later. The collar insignia worn by Gunderson are USMC overcoat buttons.

Marines near Herschbach, Germany in 1919 during the Army of Occupation.

This pontoon bridge on the Rhine is far more substantial than the flimsy footbridges thrown across the Meuse on the last night of the war, 1919.

The 80th Company lines up for chow, 1919.

C. A. Brannen was billeted in this building, the train station, for five months during Army of Occupation, 1919.

USS *George Washington* August 3, 1919.

One campsite near Rheinbrohl, Germany of the 80th Company during Army of Occupation, 1919.

An hour's rest from training for the 80th Company during Army of Occupation, 1919.

The 80th Company's bunkhouse on the rifle range during Army of Occupation, 1919.

Before the Footprints Fade

by J. P. Brannen

The Footprints

When we were boys, my brother and I shared a room and a closet. Since we had few hangables, just some overalls and winter jackets, our parents had hung three items of our father's in the extra space. These were a hobo counter and a hail buster, which were hung from nails, and his World War I uniform, which was properly suspended from a wooden hanger.

The hobo counter was a monocular item, randomly fashioned from a pair of German binoculars by a spray of bullets from a Maxim gun. To us, the fact that the hobo counter had helped to save our father's life in the war was secondary in importance to our frequent use of the item to tally our hoboes. A train passed our farm twice a day, once on the right and once on the left. My brother's hoboes were those clinging to the train as it passed going one way, and mine were those going the other. In this way we avoided unnecessary squabbling about the use of this half-excellent optical instrument. That it had saved our father's life was the source of some confusion to me, in that it gave rise to the question: Would we be alive if Dad had been killed? Discussions with the adults were not revealing, as a query of this sort was most likely to result in a "mysterious way" explanation, such as "God moves in mysterious ways his wonders to perform." The importance of this item to us was as a vision enhancer, not as a life saver. Life stretched out endlessly before me, and there was ample time to look into the deeper issues of individual existence—whether others were trapped in the uniqueness of always being the same person, and whether the colors that they saw were the same as the ones that exploded in my mind.

The hail buster was a World War I helmet. It was olive drab in color and had a 2nd Division Indian head on a white star painted on the front. No agreement had been reached between my brother and me as regarded sharing the hail buster. The chatter of summer hail on the sheet-metal roof of our house invariably led to a mad race for the closet to retrieve the hail buster and an equally disorderly dash by the winner to the front yard to dance about in glee to the accompaniment of a mighty symphony played by the hail on the helmet. The loser—usually me, as I was sometimes two and sometimes three years the younger—could only keep pace hopping up and down in frustration on the front porch. The winner always ended up sharing the hail buster, as not all the body was protected by it, the rain was almost as cold as the ice, and the hail stung what it did reach. I have recently acquired a helmet like those used by the Americans in World War I. It still protects from hail, but the sounds aren't as loud in 1993 as they were in 1933.

Dad's uniform had no obvious utilitarian value. We saw it daily, and I remember some things about it. It, like the hail buster, was olive drab in color and had a big 2nd Division patch sewn to the shoulder. There was a stripe on the lower sleeve, which I later learned was a wound stripe. Medals hung on the breast. The most interesting was the multicolored victory medal. It had five bronze clasps, each with some words engraved.[1] Actually only one was engraved with words. It said "Defensive Sector." The others were not real words. They were engraved with mysterious letters joined together. They were "Meuse Argonne," "Aisne," "Aisne Marne," and "St. Mihiel." There were things to be learned about them, but there was plenty of time. The uniform would always be there, and, with an endless life, this could be studied at leisure. Besides, if I asked Dad what it meant, the answer would almost always be, "I made some tracks around there," which was about as revealing as the "mysterious way" explanation.

Our sister, whose upcoming birth in my seventh year was responsible for much of the freedom accorded my brother and me to count hoboes and hail dance, sent Dad's memoir to the press of his university, Texas A&M, which decided to publish it. The memoir, my memories, and insights formed from remarks he made over the years are fading sources of connections with the tracks he made. He and I never had an actual conversation about his World War I experiences. An event might trigger a remark. I might ask a question, and if he wished, he would answer; if not, this unusually taciturn man would grunt.[2] Of one thing I am certain: he answered either truthfully or not at all.

Life, it turns out, is not as endless as it appeared in my seventh year. Dad is dead.[3] That fact came as a surprise to both of us, as he was very health-conscious, maybe even a health nut, and it never occurred to me that he would not eventually become known as the last surviving World War I veteran.[4] In my mind, there would be a big spread in *Life* magazine about him, just as there was about the last Civil War veteran. That was not to be. The world's finest hail dancer's failure to return from World War II led to Mother's early death. They called it cancer, but she died of a broken heart.

During my second year of high school and Dad's forty-third year of life, he went into the Marine Corps. It was 1942. I was extremely proud of him, not because he was entering the service, but because I always had been proud of him. In my younger years, it was a certainty to me that I was the envy of all the other boys for having a father like him.[5] It was years before I came to realize that it was common for children to have that feeling about their parents.

Stereotypes don't work in describing him. If he was a "gung-ho" marine, it was well concealed from me. Up until the early 1940s, I always thought that he had been in the army during the first war, and since I had no knowledge of what the Marine Corps was, I had some disappointment that he had not been in a fighting outfit. My assumption was that the army did all the fighting. It wasn't that he wished to conceal his connection with the corps; it just never came up. That I heard someone say of him, "Mister Andrew is the peculiarest man I've ever known," did not offend me. He was a loner. That does not mean he did not enjoy people; he did. What it does mean is that he was perfectly content to be alone. I don't remember ever hearing him use a swear word. And the spouses of all of his children have spoken of his gentleness. He was the easiest man to be around that I have ever known.

He took pride in his skills and abilities. Under slightly different circumstances he may have become an impressive Marine Corps leader, but he found no pleasure in telling other people what to do. In an era which had a strong component of "yelling and telling" as a leadership skill, he would have been out of place. Physically, he was five feet nine inches tall and weighed about 165 pounds. He was regarded as being an extremely handsome man, and his physique was that of a body builder, yet he did not work at it. He was rock hard. During my senior year in high school, he introduced me to some marines at the El Toro Air Station; they immediately asked if I was as hard as he. I wasn't. Once as he and I were walking toward one of the hangars at the Eagle Mountain Lake Marine Corps Air Station, we met a sergeant coming from the hangar. He and Dad wore some of the same ribbons. They both stopped, I assume there was a salute, and began a discussion of the summer of 1918. I did not intrude. Later, as Dad and I resumed our journey, I asked about the sergeant. The response was, "He was in the 5th Regiment." Not much information, but typical. If I asked his advice, the response would most likely be, "What do you think you ought to do?" His loyalty to Texas A&M University and his loyalty to the Marine Corps were deep, quiet, and complete. As one of his grandsons implied, "Both the Aggies and the marines would be better served if more of their followers had had that same kind of silent devotion."

The hail dancer had also been a student at Texas A&M, and when my turn came, I too attended that school. Shortly after the war, Dad wanted me to go with him to the Aggie Muster. In this ceremony, the names of the deceased are called out, and the answer "Here" is given. When the hail dancer's name was to be called out, he and I would answer as one. I was still in the service and stationed not far away; I could have gone but would not. Dad did not go either. If he was disappointed in my refusal to attend, he did not say so. I always knew that he did not object to my peculiarities any more than I objected to his.

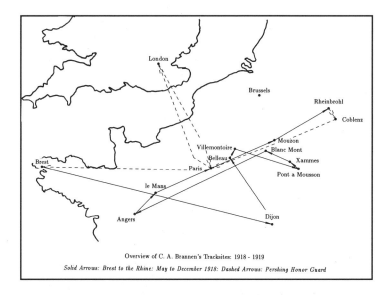

Overview of C. A. Brannen's Tracksites: 1918 - 1919

Solid Arrows: Brest to the Rhine: May to December 1918: Dashed Arrows: Pershing Honor Guard

Map 8. Overview of C. A. Brannen's Tracksites, 1918–1919. Courtesy of J. P. Brannen.

I was aware of Dad's feelings for Texas A&M but did not appreciate the depth of his feelings for the Marine Corps until near his end. He knew that his time was short and wanted to arrange an appropriate funeral. He told me that he wanted a military funeral and wanted to have a joint funeral for the hail dancer. The hail dancer was a missing-in-action case. As far as I was concerned, it did not follow that he was dead. That he had been missing for more than thirty years did not matter. He still might turn up. I was to arrange it through the local American Legion post, the one named for the hail dancer.[6] I agreed to have the services cover the hail dancer but told him, having been in the navy, I'd prefer having marines do the honors, since at least one was likely to shoot himself in the foot and thus relieve the somber tone of the upcoming occasion. He took the remark seriously and asked if I could do that. I said that if he wanted marines, then I would get some. From that point on, he told one and all that his funeral wasn't too far off and that it would be a mistake to miss such a fine show. Nothing like it had been seen around those parts. There would be marines.

Getting marines took some doing, but I did it by telling a

certain colonel that Dad always said that the marines took care of their own and that it would be a shame to send one of the last World War I marines with five battle stars to his reward by courtesy of some ill-clad, fumbling swabbies who no doubt would shoot themselves in the foot. At the funeral, the marines showed up on time and, true to Dad's promise, they put on an outstanding show. The captain joined Mother and the hail dancer in style, with a half-dozen sharp marines as sideboys.

I don't know how intelligent Dad was. He sometimes was too powerful physically for his own and sometimes for my good. A cow got down the winter of 1941, before he left for the corps in April 1942. She was sure to die if she did not get back on her feet. How the two of us got her up into a trailer I don't recall. We took her home and, amid remarks on his part about Archimedes and moving the earth with a place to stand and a long enough pole, we dug four post holes for the legs and another for his fulcrum. A long pole and a burlap sling completed my requirements for playing the role defined by the brilliant Greek. Over the next month or so, my job consisted of caring for the unfortunate animal. The ground beneath her would become foul, I would dig four more holes, lift her, and move her to her new position. In time the circle about the fulcrum was fouled. A new hole would be dug for the fulcrum, which enabled a cow lifted from the fouled circle to start a new circle tangent to the abandoned one. Before it was over, I had a half-acre of slick and slimy manure-fouled circles. The appearance of those strange geometric figures today would likely provoke an extensive cow mutilation–UFO investigation. Dad's projects weren't always fun, but they were adventures. The cow survived and sold for twenty-six dollars when he left for Quantico.

When he was turning seventy, he got it into his mind to build a hay barn down on one of the bottom fields. It was forty by twenty feet, with a roof supported by three huge beams. The beams were bridge beams discarded by the highway department. He put them in position with no assistance. As far as I know, he did not do it Archimedes style, but don't put it past him. His place to stand was his pickup truck. First he lifted a beam end to the bed, then he stood on the truck top and made a final lift to the top of the pole on which it was to rest.[7] The barn was completed, but the top of the truck had strange depressions that caused one to puzzle about a rollover accident which dented only the top. His strength stayed until almost the end.

His method of kid control was primarily by "setting the example" and clearing his throat. A "harumph" from him was sufficient to alter the undesirable behavior pattern. My sister has the honor of being the only one of us ever to receive a spanking from Dad, while I set an Olympic-style record at receiving them from Mother—close to five thousand in fourteen years. Sister was about four years old and acted up in church. Mother raised hell with Dad, so he took her home and spanked her with a three-inch pocket comb. He was so upset about it that she got ice cream and anything else that crossed her mind for the rest of his life. He wouldn't have spanked her if Mother had not been out of control.

Remarks to me about World War I usually were made while we "fixed fence." We spent many days walking those fence lines, making repairs. I never knew exactly what was going on, because a query usually elicited some remark like: "If a hair on my head knew my plans, I'd jerk it out by the roots." This statement was attributed to a particular hero of his, Gen. Stonewall Jackson. Since the operation was his, I had no control over what was going on. Once, on returning home after a long day, Mother asked what he fed me. When she learned that he was taking one of her boys out for a full day's work with no food, she laid down the law. Nobody crossed her, and so the next time we left, Dad stopped by the store and picked up a loaf of bread. When he decided it was lunch time, we sat down for our bread and water—punishment food in the navy. It was then that Dad noticed some rock salt we had for the cows and invented what became one of our staples, the salt sandwich.

He and I kept up our cow-working and fence-fixing comradeship as long as we could. We made a good team. I swung an ax from the left and he from the right. When I was larger, we could cut a tree in record time with alternating left and right strokes. After I was married, we would contrive a crisis that demanded our immediate attention. Because both he and I were employed by schools or universities, these crises would come up between Christmas and New Year's. There was the dehorning operation, during which one of his wild cows walked all over me when the gate came off at the hinges when she hit it. There was the water-gap operation when we spent a couple of days neck-deep in water at near freezing temperatures working on a cow fence.[8] There was the nine-thousand-pine-tree planting operation. While his projects may have sometimes been dangerous, I was never afraid. We both knew that if I should be injured, Mother would kick his butt. Those hours we spent in that cow operation rank in the top tier of my treasures of this life, and I never did like cows.

The house burned when Dad was back in service during World War II. It was my last year of high school, 1943–44, and Mother, sister, and I were with Dad on the West Coast. The uniform and the hail buster did not survive the fire. Dad had given the hobo counter to a local museum, and it has disappeared.

Dad's Footprints in Europe

European winds and rains of seventy-five years have erased the tracks Dad made in Europe. But in the summer of 1992, my sister, brother-in-law, and I returned to the general scenes of Dad's summer of 1918. There I discovered that, while the tracks are gone, his memoir, his records of the Great War, and the impact of his footprints on my mind were sufficient to enable me to go to places where he had been—not just to battlefield monuments and markers, but to within a very few meters of where some event notable to him, and consequently to me, took place in that summer of 1918. This led to a return in the summer of 1993, with the goal of returning to Dad's battlestar track sites and at each of these sites placing myself at a point very near to where he had been seventy-five years earlier.

Dad had gone into the Marine Corps in February 1918. Three months later he had experienced boot camp at Parris Island and a quick U-boat dodging cruise on the *Henderson* to Brest. From there he was moved to a training area near the Swiss border not far from Dijon.

In France he was trained as a light machine gunner. The marines had been equipped with an excellent British weapon, the Lewis gun, featuring a circular magazine of forty-seven rounds. In France these were traded for a French light machine gun or automatic rifle called the Chauchat. The Chauchat used a semicircular magazine of twenty rounds. It was a mechanically operated (as distinguished from gas-operated) weapon with the entire barrel slamming back on recoil. This contributed to a difficulty in maintaining accuracy. I have read that it did usually manage to work in dirt and grime, and I have read that it did not. The United States bought thirty thousand of the weapons with roughly half chambered for the French Lebel cartridge and half chambered for the U.S. rifle cartridge. The Chauchat has the distinction of being the only weapon taken in large numbers from the French by the Germans in 1940 which was not subsequently used against the Allies.

In addition to the usual rifleman training, Dad was also trained as a rifle grenadier. The rifle grenade used was the French Viven Bessiére. It was a curious weapon, consisting of a grenade slipped into a cone, the *tromblon,* fitted over the rifle barrel. It was projected by firing a round through the center of the grenade. The bullet, when passing through the grenade, ignited a seven-second fuze while the gases and bullet impact propelled the grenade. The butt of the rifle was placed against the ground, with the trajectory determined by the barrel elevation. Range was fifty to seventy-five yards.

Although Dad never mentioned it, one can determine from his various assignments that his specialized training was for employment in the squad which provided light machine gunners, runners, and grenadier support for the company. This was an adaptation of the so-called "suicide squad" developed by the British during the preceding years of warfare.

As Dad trained, Ludendorff launched his offensive in the spring of 1918. In short order, he had given Soissons to the Kaiser, and, if only he could take Reims and its rail junction, logistical problems would be much easier to manage. Near Paris, the front was somewhat U-shaped with the open arms to the northeast and full of Germans. Soissons was on the upper portion of the northern arm, and Reims was near the midpoint of the southern arm. At the base, on the banks of the Marne, was the town of Château-Thierry. Nearby was a small wood associated with the village of Belleau. Actually the forest had been some noble's hunting preserve.

The Germans crossed the Marne, causing some panic among the Paris politicians. Pershing offered and Foch accepted two of the American divisions to check the German advance. These divisions had been in training along quiet sectors of the front. The 2nd Division was made up of the 4th Brigade (the Marine brigade, consisting of the 5th and 6th Regiments), the 3rd Brigade (the Army brigade, made up of the 9th and 23rd Infantry Regiments), and the 2nd Field Artillery Brigade. This division was sent to the Château-Thierry area. The Marine brigade was given the forest near Belleau to clear. On June 6, they attacked across a wheat field and sustained losses of around 50 percent. Replacements were rushed in from the training camps to bolster the strength of the depleted companies.

Battle Star: Belleau Wood

Dad entered the Belleau Wood action on June 8, as one of 213 men from replacement Battalion 138. He was attached to the 80th Company, 6th Regiment of marines. This was a company of the 2nd Battalion—the Holcomb Battalion. Colonel Lee, the regimental commander, wrote to the Marine Corps commandant, Major General Barnett in Washington, of the "remarkable conduct" of Dad and his fellow "raw replacements."

Dad was assigned to the platoon of Lieutenant Overton. Overton was one of ten senior students commissioned directly from Yale into the Marine Corps in April 1917. By the time Dad joined his platoon, Overton, a native of Nashville, had more than a year's service as an officer. He was an outstanding leader and commanded the company for much of the battle of Belleau Wood after Captain Coffenberg was wounded and evacuated. He handled the company with great skill and was one of the outstanding young officers commissioned by the Marine Corps during the spring and summer of 1917. Several future commandants of the corps were in that class of young officers. Dad had great respect for Lieutenant Overton, and if the sibling born during my seventh summer had been a boy, he would have been named for Lieutenant Overton.

Very shortly after Dad joined the 80th Company, its position was just north and west of the village of Bouresches. The village had been captured by the 96th Company earlier in the battle. The beauty of Bouresches was that somewhere it contained a well, and Dad, out of water and thirsty, learned of the well. He collected canteens from his companions and managed, between shell bursts, to fill the canteens. My sister, brother-in-law, and I found that well site in the summer of 1992. It was behind a nonfunctioning lion's-head fountain along a wall near the center of the village. The water was rich in algae. When I returned in July 1993, the water was gone, but the sign proclaiming that place as the village firefighting reservoir was still there. Originally we found that lion's head not through an adult but through a child of hail-dancing age who overheard our efforts to communicate with an adult.[9]

From a study of the maps of the battle in Asprey's *At Belleau Wood*, it was easy to stand beside the road from Bouresches to Lucy-le-Bocage and follow with the eye and mind the path Dad took from the edge of the forest to the village. The inset of the 2nd Division Operations map shows the 2nd and 6th positions from June 13–17. The trip Dad made to the well is consistent with the trek having been made from that position of the 80th Company.

Dad's last machine-gun position at Belleau Wood overlooked what became the American cemetery. This he had mentioned in his memoir. Since his memoir was written in the 1930s, I asked myself how he had known that. Perhaps there was an early photograph or, more likely, he returned to the battlefield a year later, while in Paris as a member of the composite regiment called the Pershing Honor Guard. At that time Lieutenant Overton, whose body was returned to Nashville in 1923, was buried there, and Dad would have visited the grave. In those days Bouresches was on a rail line.

The attack made by the 2nd Battalion between June 12 and 15 appears to have taken place right behind the present monument. At times during his three weeks in Belleau Wood, Dad had been to the right or south of the line from Lucy-le-Bocage to Belleau, but toward the end he would have been more in the center. Thus, by standing behind the monument, on the noncemetery side, and looking toward the village of Belleau, I was looking not over what he saw, but at least from where he saw whatever he did see.

Among the Battle Monument Commission people, a story is told of a German who for years came at intervals to an American cemetery and there placed flowers on the grave of a certain man. Eventually someone asked if the American was a relative.

"No," was the reply, "I killed him."

"Then you regret having killed him."

"No, his bullets were seeking me when mine found him."

The road from Lucy-le-Bocage to Belleau, which lies north of the forest, passes a German cemetery.

As I walked among the markers, I wondered which was the sniper whose concealment in a tree was compromised by a patch of sunlight that fell on his face. And which was the courier who was felled by long-range Chauchat fire as he pedaled along the road to Belleau. If I had known, I would have placed flowers on their graves in Dad's memory.

Dad never said to me that he had killed these two men. However, faintly recalled enigmatic remarks implied that he remembered them.[10] Then, too, there was his remarkable eyesight and marksmanship. In 1942 he fired first and second with pistol and rifle from an officer group of four hundred at Quantico.

Finally, I cannot leave the subject of Belleau without paying homage to the bulldog fountain near the mayor's office. The young lady at the visitor's center at the cemetery said that this was where the marines got their bulldog mascot motif. The Germans named the marines "Devil Dogs," or, more precisely, "Hounds from Hell." But why a bulldog? Perhaps she was correct.

Battle Star: Soissons

The 2nd Division was relieved on July 5, but eleven days later they were being rushed north by *camions* to join Mangin's Tenth Army. Ludendorff had launched a major attack on July 15, with the objective of taking Reims. Foch, despite the pleas of Pétain, held the Tenth in reserve. As Ludendorff pushed on the lower portion of the bulge, Mangin lurked on his right flank between Paris and Soissons. Foch rushed the U.S. 1st and 2nd Divisions to beef up the Tenth. The Americans arrived at their designated positions literally minutes before they participated in a massive Allied counterattack launched on July 18.

This attack was carried out with the support of 233 French tanks, including three models: the obsolete St. Chamont and Schneider heavy tanks and the Ft 17 light tank. The U.S. divisions were sandwiched between French divisions which, from north to south, were: French division, 1st U.S. Division, Moroccan division, 2nd U.S. Division, 38th French division. The 5th Marines led the 4th Brigade attack, with the 6th held as corps reserve. During the day, the 5th, 9th, and 23rd Regiments of the 4th Brigade gained some ten kilometers from their starting line through the Forest of Retz. The 5th fought through the ravine at Vierzy and stopped, with the end of day, to the east of the village. The Germans were surprised but fell back in some semblance of order and, during the night of the 18th, rushed reinforcements down from Soissons.

Mangin sensed an opportunity for great advance and asked Pétain for more troops. Pétain, ever cautious, sensed that about all that could be accomplished had been done and hoarded his reserves. Mangin threw in his, the 6th Regiment. Meanwhile he covered himself by going around Pétain to let Foch know what he had done.

The 6th Regiment was assigned a broad front that on the 18th had been covered by three regiments. They advanced from their reserve position through the ravine at Vierzy and formed their front with the 2nd Battalion in the old French trenches southwest of Charantigny. The attack began at about 8:30 A.M. and slammed right into a German counterattack in preparation. The 2nd Battalion was on the left and the 1st on the right, with the 3rd in reserve. The 2nd Battalion attacked on a two-company front, with the 78th and 79th leading. In the second wave, the 96th Company was to the left. The 80th, Dad's company, was next to the 96th. The Moroccans were to the immediate left of the 2nd Battalion. There was little artillery support for the 6th, while it in turn was subjected to intensive machine-gun and artillery fire. In short order, the company suffered 120 casualties. Twenty-five of them, including Lieutenant Overton, died. Dad found himself alone far in advance of the company, where he was pinned in a "sunken road" by a German machine gunner all day long. I wanted to find that road and what I came to regard as the Cates' trench.

I was not optimistic about our chances of finding the site where the 2nd Battalion had been. The clues were few. I did not find maps in the Map Archives in Alexandria, Virginia. From an unsigned account of the marines in World War I, I learned that the 2nd Battalion reached the shelter of the woods some five hundred yards west of Villemontoire. An unsigned 96th Company history states that the company dug in with its left on the Vierzy-Raperie Road, approximately three kilometers east of Vierzy, near Villemontoire. Toland states of Cates at

Soissons: "He gathered what men he could, about 20 of them, took refuge in trenches near an old sugar mill, and waited for an enemy counterattack." The last clue was that I had once asked Dad if his company had attained its objective at Soissons. He replied that they had not, but that he saw it. Since the objective was the Soissons–Château-Thierry highway, wherever the sunken road might be, it had to be in sight of the highway. Fortunately, the highway had not moved in seventy-five years. The key became finding the World War I–era sugar beet mill near Villemontoire. I also knew that the 1st Battalion had been unable to advance beyond Tigny.

With all these things in mind, I had the following sentence translated into French by a saleslady in Paris: In the year 1917, where was sugar manufactured? She recorded in my notebook: "S'il vous plaît, où se trouvaient das l'annèe 1917 les champs de betteraves à sucre?"[11] A French source said it should have been: "S'il vous plaît, où se trouvaient pendant l'année 1918 les champs de betteraves à sucre."

On the morning of May 6, we left De Gaulle Airport hoping to arrive that evening at a hotel in Blèrancourt, a village northwest of Soissons. An interim stop was to be the Soissons battlefield. The plan was first to pass through the forest of Villers-Cotterêts, where the 2nd Division joined Mangin's Tenth Army for the July 18 attack. From there we would go to the ravine at Vierzy and proceed to the villages of Tigny and Villemontoire.

The forest of Villers-Cotterêts turned out to have a somewhat dark and forbidding appearance, making it a suitable locale for the activities of one of its better-known sons, the original Bluebeard. Toland states that many scholars give this forest as the hideout of the fifteenth-century monster. While still within the forest, we passed a sign pointing to "Mon. Mangin." We passed it by and continued toward the Vierzy turnoff. In retrospect, I regret not going to that monument, as it was the site at which Mangin had his engineers construct a wooden tower twenty meters high, from which he could observe the attack on the 18th. Pétain had chastised him for being out of touch atop that tower, but Mangin pointed out his staff and gallopers below and told his superior that he was in touch.

Beyond the forest we came to a monument commemorating the counterattack launched by the Tenth Army on July 18. Beyond that was a small British cemetery. For me, the surprising discovery was that there were several sets of side-by-side graves in groups of seven. Each group of men had died on the same date. They were air crewmen from World War II. In addition, the air crew position of each was given. Since the correspondence between the dead and Lancaster crew positions was one to one, I concluded that these were Lancaster air crews lost in Britain's bomber offensive. The World War I servicemen buried there had died before the Aisne-Marne offensive of 1918.

Our first search was for the woods five hundred meters west of Villemontoire. There were woods there along a ravine. We tramped about a recently planted sugar beet field. I picked up a cartridge hull with that tapered shape of the powder section characteristic of the Lebel used in the Chauchat gun. But things did not feel right. We drove to the village of Villemontoire. No one was around. At last we found a young lady, Stephanie Van Ruymbeke. We showed her our sentence. She pointed toward Tigny. We made a brief stop at a British cemetery on the road to Tigny. The British soldiers were from the 15th Scottish Division and most had died in late July or early August of 1918.[12]

At Tigny we discovered a 2nd Division marker on the outskirts of the village. It consisted of a cast bronze plaque mounted on a large boulder. About it was a well-tended flower garden with the flowers in bloom.[13] While it was nice to find the marker, there was still disquiet regarding the location of what I had come to think of as Dad's place.

We came upon a pair of men working in the yard of the headquarters of a farming operation. We showed them our sentence. All we got out of them was, "Patron." The patron showed up with wife and daughter—the family Doncoeur. Both mother and daughter spoke excellent English. They were a veritable gold mine of information. The patron showed us a photocopy of a map the family had acquired from the Americans. It was from something like a U.S. War Graves Commission map. It had a note on it pinpointing the temporary burial sites of two privates, Cox and Corey, from the 83rd Company, 6th Marines. The 83rd Company was in the 3rd Battalion. In response to our question about the ruins of a sugar beet mill, the family directed us to the Parcy part of the Commune of Tigny-Parcy. They also showed us an aerial photo of the ruins of Tigny in 1918.

Parcy lies at the end of the ravine that passes through Vierzy.

Things did not feel right. If Cates' trench was there, then a future commandant of the corps was a long way from where he should have been. I was discouraged. We left the area.

Several days later, we returned. I began to reexamine the old and new clues. The 3rd Battalion was in reserve for the 6th Regiment. The left end of the 2nd Division was around that British cemetery. Dad could see the highway before he sought shelter in the sunken road. The map given us by the Doncoeurs showed the line at the end of the day on July 19. By this time, I had concluded that this map was our best source of information for Soissons. I walked from the region of the 2nd Battalion attack toward the Soissons–Château-Thierry road, trying to focus on how far Dad had to go before he saw the highway. I had to conclude that he could not see the highway until well east of the Tigny–Villemontoire road, as the intervening rising terrain blocked the view.

During this time, the three of us were tramping around in the planted fields. Those west of the Tigny–Villemontoire road were planted in sugar beets. Those east of the road were planted in fodder of some type, maybe a plant similar to maize. There was one tractor road through a field that caught my sister's attention. It led to a wooded section which was of interest to me as the possible location of the machine gunner who was plinking at Dad for most of the day.[14] While there, the patron of Villemontoire, Gêrard Moquet, drove up in a pickup. He made it clear that he would like for us to come with him. We went with him to his home. Young Stephanie Van Ruymbeke had mentioned our being there several days before, and he wished to help. Madame Moquet spoke excellent English. The couple seemed pleased to have found us and provided invaluable information.[15]

The village changed hands seven times during the first war. In the past, the principal crop had been the *betterave*, the sugar beet. Now the farm included about eighty head of beef cattle and fodder was raised for them. The planting was about half fodder and half sugar beets. Prior to the first war, a sugar beet mill had been located at the crossroads where the British cemetery was now. The cobblestoned mill yard was a convenient place for composting the manure of the eighty cattle and in mid-July was slightly "nosesome."

Cates wasn't lost. I concluded that the trench could be located and that the road where Dad had found shelter that long day was clearly identified. The Soissons puzzle was solved; at least I thought it was. Not knowing better, I placed Cates' trench alongside the mill ruins and Dad's position as between the ruins and the major highway.

After returning home, an additional clue came to light. It was a report by Cates that he was holding a trench 350 yards from the mill ruins. Thus it was clear that the position I had selected on the previous trip was in error. Cates' position was several hundred yards west of the mill. From the Graves Commission map and the 350-yard distance given by Cates, it seemed clear that Dad had mistaken the road between Villemontoire and Tigny as the Soissons–Château-Thierry highway. To see the major highway, one must be several hundred meters east of the mill ruins. Under these conditions, such a mistake would be understandable. It is unlikely that Dad had even seen a map.

The French topographic map shows a small copse located approximately 370 meters west of the British cemetery. Since the 96th Company history states that the company was to the left and Cates states that his trench bordered the road, I concluded that the Cates' trench ran through the small copse. We had examined that place on our 1992 visit. It was uninviting, with boulders heaped about; and my sister remarked that it looked like a place where bad things went on.

Following my second trip to the site in 1993, I wrote to the Doncoeurs seeking permission to use their names in this account and to seek information about the aerial photo of Tigny. Finally, I wanted information about the map they had given me. I sent them a copy of what I had written about Dad at Soissons. In time, I received correspondence from Mr. Gaston, a World War I collector-historian whose specialties include at least the Americans and the Soissons battle. He and his colleague Mr. Dehé have a library of about a thousand out-of-print books or documents. This information base is extensive, and Gaston was able to verify my general positioning of Dad on July 19. Additional information from him straightened out my errors.

Gaston possesses a marvelous tenacity for accuracy. I would

be surprised to find an error of mine that had escaped him. To begin with, he pointed out that Bluebeard's action was not in the forest of Villers-Cotterêts as Toland had stated but took place near Nantes.

He went on to point out that Bluebeard was the Baron Gilles de Rais, and the alternate writing of Rais is Retz. However, it is not related to the forest of Retz which is the alternate name for the forest of Villers-Cotterêts.

Gaston pointed out that Dad did not need to be as far east as I had thought to see the Soissons–Château Thierry highway as in the summer of 1918 the road was lined with large trees. In addition he included a topographic map from a French book *Le combat d'une division* by Colonel Loizeau. This map shows the trenches, the wire panels, and the positions and fields of fire of the German machine guns. Loizeau was chief of staff of the French 58th Division which relieved the 2nd U.S. Division on the night of July 19. Included was a panoramic sketch of the view approximately from Cates' position.

Gaston also sent photocopies of two messages relevant to the position of Cates in the trench. The messages are as follows:

> *From: 2nd Bn. 6th Regt.*
> *At: Road bed about 178.4–286.4.*
> *Date: July 19, 1918. Hour 10:23 A.M.*
> *To: Lt. Col. Lee.*

The text of the message does not impact my search but the heading gives map coordinates 178.4–286.4. The message from Cates to Holcomb:

> *From Co. "H"*
> *At: ?*
> *Date: July 19. Hour 10:45 A.M.*
> *To: Major Holcomb.*
>
> *I am in an old abandoned French trench bordering on road leading out from your P.C. and 350 yds. from an old mill. I have only two men out of my company. We need support, but it is almost suicide to try and get it here as we are swept by machine-gun fire and a constant barrage is on us. I have no one on my left and only a few on my right. I will hold.*
>
> > *Cates*
> > *2nd Lt. 96 Co.*

Although the military coordinates are not shown on the map adapted from that provided by Gaston, they are on the original and enable a precise location of both Holcomb's P.C., Post of Command, and Cates' position in the trench. Move east for Dad's "some hundred yards" and that is his position. A cut is shown on the French map, and it is there today. The width of the road enables the gunner atop Hill 157 some five hundred meters away to keep Dad pinned down for the day. These positions are indicated on the map titled 2nd Villemontoire-Tigny Region. Other things I learned from Gaston included:

1. Gaston's opinion of Lieutenant Overton is consistent with mine and Dad's. Gaston sent a copy of a letter from Lieutenant Meeks, one of the Yale lieutenants, to Overton's parents. Meeks gave the letter to the superintendent of the American cemetery at Belleau Wood. Meeks and a companion buried Overton on the evening of the nineteenth. There was the obligatory sentence regarding absence of pain and suffering.

2. The map copied for us by the Doncoeurs came from the leader of an American Graves Commission party searching for the graves of Cox and Corey of the 83rd Company. It turns out that in the early 1980s, a man named Scarborough of the 83rd became concerned about two of his comrades who had been buried at Soissons and who apparently were still missing. He drew the position of the graves as he remembered them. A search was undertaken to find those graves. The map also had a note suggesting that the graves contained enough cartridge brass to trigger a metal detector. Gaston helped with the search. Incidentally, the graves of Cox and Corey were not found, and Gaston was of the opinion that they were disinterred by the Americans and buried as missing. Apparently it was common for U.S. soldiers to discard their dog tags to preclude the possibility of their clicking together and so revealing a soldier's presence on night patrol. Dad did not discard his. We still have them. The aluminum discs had been placed sufficiently far apart on their string to avoid touching (or clicking). I assume that Cox and Corey had discarded theirs. Along this line, Meeks mentioned in his letter that he had removed *both* of Overton's dog tags. Why? The reason for two was so one could be left with the body and the other be given to Graves Registration.

3. Gaston pointed out that the Moroccan division called

the 1st on the U.S. map was the only Moroccan division at that time and that the use of 1st was not appropriate. He also mentioned the fame of the division. I assume that some of that fame came from their role in the recapture of Fort Douamount at Verdun.

4. The location of Holcomb's P.C. [Post of Command] also enabled me to locate the sugar beet field that loomed so large in Dad's memory. Holcomb's P.C. was in a sugar beet field as "Major Denig was in a beet field desperately digging with a spade he had picked up, while shrapnel rained about him. Holcomb asked if he could borrow it for a while. Denig said yes, when his hole was deep enough."[16] I assume this is the same beet field where some of the 80th Company passed over and some, Overton and Red Williams at least, did not. Exactly seventy-five years later that field was again in beets.

5. Gaston quite logically takes issue with my placement of Dijon near Switzerland. Since the distance is 120 kilometers, the word *near* is not appropriate. He is correct, of course, from the European viewpoint. In my world, where towns are farther apart than that, the word *near* is appropriate.

Battle Star: St. Mihiel

Following the frightful losses at Soissons, the 2nd Division was out of work for over a month. The units were brought back up to strength through replacements and by the return of some of the wounded from Belleau Wood and Soissons. Among the returning wounded of Belleau Wood was Dad's buddy Scatterbrain. The nickname must have been appropriate, as Dad remarked a number of times on the antics of Scatterbrain. Surprisingly enough, I don't remember any of them. In contrast, we learned after Dad's death that his own nickname was Noisy, no doubt a reference to his taciturn nature. In addition, a new platoon commander, Lt. David R. Kilduff, transferred in from the 96th Company.

On the other side of the line, Ludendorff saw his blackest day, August 8, when the British attacked along the northern part of his overextended front. Meanwhile, Pershing was putting together an army of sixteen divisions for an all-American effort to reduce the St. Mihiel salient. This was a bulge in the line southeast of Verdun. Pershing launched his attack on September 12.

The 2nd Division advance began around Remenauville and by the end of the day had moved beyond Thiaucourt some six kilometers to the northeast. Early on the morning of September 15, the 80th Company was leading the battalion, with the Kilduff platoon out front. Near dawn a German was surprised and captured. Major Williams, who had taken over the battalion command from Holcomb, called a halt and sent the Kilduff platoon ahead to reconnoiter. The platoon moved across a small clearing, and Noisy and Scatterbrain, uncomfortable with the exposure, drifted over to the right for cover. The platoon was unexpectedly hit hard by machine gun fire. Some of the men in the clearing who were not hit brought Kilduff, who was down, over to the area where Noisy and Scatterbrain had cover. Kilduff's wound was mortal.

Scatterbrain, poking about in the underbrush, looked over a bluff and discovered a large number of Germans below, moving toward the platoon. He summoned Noisy, and together the pair, who were carrying VB rifle grenades and had a good supply, began working the Germans over. Under this attack, the enemy retreated over a ridge. Scatterbrain was awarded a silver star for his activities that day.

My goal at St. Mihiel was to find the locale of the Kilduff ambush. On my first trip, the clues were too few. All I knew was that the 4th Brigade was between the villages of Xammes and Jaulny. At that time I had not examined the actions of the brigade or the battalion sufficiently to pick up on its custom of placing the 5th Regiment on the right and the 6th on the left, or on the 6th Regiment's habit of having the 2nd Battalion on the left and the 1st on the right (if one of these latter was held in reserve, the 3rd took its place). Consequently, I had no likely place to look between the two villages, which are some three kilometers apart.

Additional information was available from the study of a 1918 map of the area at 1:1000 scale. This, surprisingly, was held in the map room of the University of New Mexico. It was the only such French map there, and it covered the two small villages. How the university came to hold only this 1918 map must be an interesting story in its own right. I scrutinized the map, seeking a bluff for Scatterbrain to peer over and a ridge for the surprised Germans to disappear behind. The most promising spot was near Jaulny.

After stopping at the U.S. cemetery near Thiaucourt and finding Kilduff's marker, we drove up toward Jaulny to the spot I had selected. It certainly looked promising, but there was nothing definite.

Before returning on the seventy-fifth anniversary, I came into possession of a 6th Regiment history which supplemented my clue larder considerably. The best clue was an order to Major Williams at 3 A.M. on September 15. He was to "proceed up the Xammes-Charey road to X-line 244.3 and Hill 231.5 and deploy along the undeveloped road going into the forest."

Fortunately, the 1918 1:10000 map and a current French 1:25000 topographical map show the unimproved road associated with Hill 231.5 to be unchanged. Nor has the Xammes-Charey road been moved. On my second trip to the area, I found, at about twelve hundred meters toward Charey from Xammes, a small clearing to the left of the road, perhaps an acre in size. To the right was the unimproved road which drops to a stream bed south of Hill 231.5. The small clearing lay next to a modest holding yard for gravel and other road repair materials. The clearing was one or two meters higher than the road, with the road materials depot excavated out at road level. The clearing did not appear to be the result of clear-cutting the forest. Instead it was suggestive of one of those ecological surprises that one sometimes finds in deep forests.

To the right of the clearing was a bluff overlooking the stream bed south of Hill 231.5. Beyond the stream was a ridge. Putting Dad's observations and Williams' orders together, I concluded that the clearing was the ambush site.

On the map 6th Marines at St. Mihiel, the clearing is indicated by Kilduff Plt. Hill 231.5 and is labeled Kompanie Konrad. About six hundred meters further along the road toward Charey, a narrow macadam road branched off to the northeast. This was beyond the forest, in open farmland. About a kilometer along this road, almost to the road from Rembercourt-sur-Mad, stood a concrete bunker. The 1918 map shows this to be part of the Hindenburg line. This is also the area from which the

Germans launched strong counterattacks against the 2nd Division. The bunker is on the unimproved road just beyond the curve and goes to Mon Plaisir Farm.

Battle Star: Blanc Mont

The 2nd Division was hurt at St. Mihiel, but not as badly as at Belleau Wood and Soissons. It was relieved on September 16 and spent ten days in refurbishments. Once again, as at Soissons, it was loaned to the French. This time it was to assist in the reduction of a key German position on Blanc Mont Ridge in the Champagne sector. The Germans had held this high ground since 1914, and many lives had been lost on both sides in French efforts to take it. The Germans had constructed formidable positions along the ridge and had not neglected the undulating terrain rising from the French positions three kilometers away, along the railway at the bottom. The strength of the German positions is indicated by the fact that it was selected as the site from which the Kaiser observed Ludendorff's July 15 assault near Reims. The Champagne chalk had been digesting divisions for four years and was, according to one marine, "a place just built for calamities."[17] Among the tragedies of the war, the French accord these battles near Blanc Mont a status just after those of Verdun.

The French were delighted to obtain the big American division, almost twice the size of theirs, and immediately began making plans to break it into smaller units that would be easier to assimilate into their own units. The Marine Corps General Lejeune, who was now commanding the 2nd Division, circumvented the breakup by promising the French Corps Commander Gouraud that the 2nd would take the ridge. Gouraud agreed, and on October 3, the 2nd Division set about the task.

The 6th Regiment led off for the 4th Brigade, with the 2nd Battalion in the lead. The company array was, left to right, 96th, 78th, 80th, and 79th. Dad's job during this attack was to serve as a runner between the 78th and the 80th. The regimental objective was Hill 210, west at the top of the ridge. In between lay three kilometers of well-fortified Champagne chalk. The 78th Company had one of the more difficult chores. There was a trench on a rise which the French never had succeeded in attacking. It was called "the Essen hook." Since it was on the

78th's immediate left, they first had to reduce it. They did so, and movement up the hill continued. Within three hours, they took the ridge itself. Somewhere on that hill, Dad took a pair of field glasses from the body of a German officer. These later saved his life by deflecting bullets and survived to become useful in hobo counting.

Two men of the 78th were awarded the Medal of Honor for their work that day, and Dad's friend Sherwood of the 80th Company was awarded a Silver Star for his. Once, when Dad and I were fixing fence, I asked him the name of the man who was killed when he was hit. Without hesitation, he said, "Pruitt." And when I asked where he was hit, Dad said that he had been hit in the face. At the time I was fairly young and did not accept the anonymous death of Dad's companion. His name should be remembered. In preparing this work, I discovered that a Pruitt of the 78th Company was awarded the Medal of Honor. On reading further, I learned that this Pruitt was killed by artillery fire. But, in the 78th Company muster roll for that month, I read that Pruitt had died of a gunshot wound in the right jaw. I don't know what the truth is. But, as I said earlier, if Dad said it, it was either the truth or he thought it was. Another possibility is that the spring in my steel-trap mind has weakened with age.

I knew there wasn't much chance that I could find the exact spot where Dad was wounded. I located the road where the 2nd Battalion lined up and the general area where he had been hit.

The ridge called Blanc Mont lies some four kilometers north of the village of Sommepy-Tahure, alongside road D320, which goes to St.-Etienne-á-Arnes. The road we took in 1992 made several right-angle turns, and at one of them, a small bakery lay dead ahead. To the right was a church much elevated above the road. On the western slope of the church mound, beside the stairway, was a small marker in French which commemorated the 2nd Division actions nearby. On the northern slope of the church grounds were several preserved fortifications employed by the Germans.

The front had been four kilometers to the south of Sommepy-Tahure from July 1915 to September 1918. The French had taken the village and turned the dugouts by the church into an aid station. I suppose this was initially used as an aid station by the Americans from October 3 to 6 and was where Dad had his wounds examined.[18] On the sixth the 2nd Division headquarters was moved here. Prior to that time, division headquarters were between the villages of Souain and Sommepy at the Wagram dugout. I assume that the name came from Napoleon's victory at Wagram, a village near Vienna in 1809.

As we continued on toward the ridge, we came to a marker erected by the 2nd Division shortly after the war. It was at a sharp turn in the road, about eight hundred meters from the village. By my map readings, the famous Essen trench lay west of the marker, at the end of the unimproved road to the west.

There was an American monument atop Hill 210. The trouble was that there were two Hill 210s, and the one we visited in 1992 was the one to the east, that was taken by the 3rd Brigade. Dad, in the company of the 4th Brigade, was on the one to the west.

In July of the seventy-fifth anniversary year, I returned to the site and went to the western Hill 210. In the exact place I wanted to visit was a French military exclusion area. It seemed that the French military had taken advantage of the height to place a communications installation there. A copse slightly to the west of the military installation merited a visit. Unfortunately, it was raining, and all the stories about the Champagne chalk mud are true. In trying to get there, I managed to bog down enough that I discarded the notion. The maps of 1918 and 1993 were consistent, however. The road from the eastern 210 to the western 210 was the one on which the 2nd Battalion was lining up when Dad left to have his side "painted."

The young pines atop the ridge which Dad mentioned still clustered around the monument and had much the same appearance as they did in archival photos taken in 1918. The places where Dad must have been were now covered by open farmland, the military exclusion area, and patches of forest. The road along which the 2nd Battalion lined up on October 3, 1918, was the one which now ran alongside the military exclusion area.

Of the Blanc Mont battle, a marshal of France was to comment: "The taking of Blanc Mont Ridge is the greatest single achievement of the 1918 campaign."

Battle Star: Meuse-Argonne

From Blanc Mont, Dad went to a hospital at Angers. There

it was determined that there was no bullet in the ragged tears in the flesh below the heart.[19] After a few weeks, he was sent to le Mans, where he was re-equipped with clothing and the accouterments of war. On his way to rejoin the 80th Company, he was given an overnight stay in Paris. He spent the entire day in the Louvre. He was so taken by the art that he missed lunch. After that brief respite, he was on his way back to his unit.

As Dad was working his way back, the 2nd Division completed its tasks around Blanc Mont Ridge and was moving to join the American army for employment in the Meuse Argonne. The 6th Regiment left the Champagne by *camions,* and, during the afternoon of October 25, Dad caught up with them as they disembarked just outside the village of Les Islettes.

Over the next two weeks, the 2nd Division moved some fifty kilometers to the north, fighting most of the way. On the night of November 10, the 6th Regiment, reinforced by one battalion from the 5th Regiment, was scheduled to force a crossing of the Meuse at the village of Mouzon, which lies between Stenay and Sedan.[20] The bridge at Mouzon had been destroyed, and much of the effort of that night was absorbed in trying to get footbridges across. The site of this crossing was the intersection of the canal with the main channel, north of the bridge site. Dad was present at the point at which the footbridges were to be placed. It was my impression, based on a comment he once made as we worked on a water gap, that he had been employed as a swimmer in the effort. The Germans were successful in preventing a crossing by the 6th that night. This was the only place in the Meuse Argonne which fit my wish to return to sites at which Dad had been and which had held some significance to him. His position on the last night of the war suited my purposes excellently. Not only was his life preserved, but, in addition, mine was made possible.

Originally, the exact site of the crossing effort was uncertain. One account suggested that the effort had been made one mile north of Mouzon. That does not seem plausible, as that was beyond the 2nd Division boundary. The most reliable site locale is given in the 2nd Division history, placing the effort by the canal juncture. Mouzon lay just off highway D964, between Stenay and Sedan. The bridge of interest was on highway D4, which simply led from Mouzon into the surrounding farmland. The bridge was undistinguished, and, at the time I was there, July, the Meuse was quite calm. A photo taken from the west side of the bridge site in 1918 shows swirling water and a twin-spired church. To the right is a building like a warehouse near the water's edge. Seventy-five years later, both church and building were still present and easily recognized. The canal cut lay only one hundred or so meters to the north of the bridge. The canal opens to the east about two hundred meters north of the bridge. It rejoins the Meuse only a few hundred meters beyond. The canal is not used today and the remains of a small lock, large enough for only barges, opens on the site of the crossing effort. It is accessible from the east. Though the river is narrow, its banks are not steep.

I puzzled over the question of how Dad could have been in the water, as the 3rd Battalion had the honor of being scheduled to cross first. As I learned to expect, Mr. Gaston came to the rescue. He sent me a detailed map of the Mouzon crossing attempt and a copy of a report by Major Shuler stating that forty marines had been detailed to help repair the footbridges which had been hit by artillery fire. Since Shuler was the 3rd Battalion commander, why would Dad have been among that crew? Perhaps he was back in the runner business and was with the 3rd for the crossing. On the other hand, Major Williams' failure to write about assigning some of his men to bridge repair does not mean that he did not do so.

The detailed report of Major Shuler stated that the assualt troops were assembled at the Mouzon railroad yard. The yard is still there, perhaps the tracks are used as a siding—certainly nothing more; the station is a home.

The 5th Regiment, with reinforcement from the 89th Division, did succeed in crossing the river to the south of Mouzon. Their casualties were heavy.

In the anniversary year, I drove south of Mouzon along the Meuse to Villemontry, which is mentioned as a 2nd Battalion location. Further along the unlabeled road from Villemontry to Létanne, I passed the site where the 5th Regiment forced its crossing on the night of November 10.

Rheinbrohl

Dad never had said very much about being in Germany, other than remarks such as one to the effect that it was easier to understand the German language than the French. However, a photo album of his turned up after he died. That was the first time I saw it. It was mostly about his time in Germany and his being stationed at Rheinbrohl.

I wanted to visit Rheinbrohl, and, as long as I was going, I would revisit a statue in the village of Schmitten, near Frankfurt. The statue had struck a chord with me when I first had come upon it many years earlier. It is a copy of one by a German sculptress mother who lost her son in World War I. Many copies were made, and supposedly they are easy to find. This happens to be the only one that I have come upon in my wanderings.

On the drive to Rheinbrohl I detoured by Azincourt and Waterloo. Azincourt was worthwhile, but Waterloo was a mistake. I was unprepared for the Disneyland-like atmosphere.

Dad on his march to Rheinbrohl had passed through a bit of Belgium and had crossed the Rhine at Bad Hönnigen. He had crossed in a motor boat with several others, probably a squad, to set up security for the passage of the battalion. I was able to cross at the same place by ferry.

Rheinbrohl lies a few kilometers upriver—south—from Bad Hönnigen. I arrived there on a Sunday morning and thus was able to wander about the village free of shopping crowds. I knew nothing of exactly where Dad had been, but I did know that he certainly had seen the castle Arenfels across the river. Also, he had to have seen the church.

I wandered about the streets and came upon a decorated *Rathaus,* or bar, which proudly proclaimed that it had been there since the year 877. Dad had to have seen that, and, if the building was a Rathaus in 1918–19, most likely he visited it.

Reflections

I cannot easily comprehend the desire to return to sites at which events of some significance occurred. The urge is more emotional than logical and seems to be shared by many of us; else, why are there historical markers? Perhaps it has to do with time and place. The passage of time is not yet reversible, but the places are still there. The scars left on the earth by the trenches of World War I were as unlike the trenches which formed them as body scars are unlike the bloody wounds which cause them. Most of the men who went to that war were born in the nineteenth century, and their body scars are mostly gone. The trenches and the remains of strong points could still be found in the wooded areas around the battle sites, and I wanted to see them. I cannot explain why.

There have been times when I have envied Dad. He was born into a world little changed from frontier days. It was a world of kerosene lamps, wood stoves, horses, and cows. He remembered seeing his first motor car and his first *aeroplane*, as it was spelled in those days. Before he died, through the magic of television, he saw men on the moon. But my greatest envy was for his integrity and character, and I think World War I had something to do with that. You might think that all one has to do to feel that character from the inside is just do it. But I have to think about it. I think it was as natural to Dad as his phenomenal eyesight and marksmanship. In fact, the most striking thing about him to me was his naturalness.

Dad used to speak of his "split-second aggressiveness." That usually came up following recovery from falling asleep at the wheel. It was a frequent occurrence and got him surveyed out of the Marine Corps in 1944. He was driving with a group of officers from Camp Gillespie to Laguna Beach. He fell asleep at the wheel. Unfortunately, a flight surgeon–type officer was aboard, and Dad was subjected to a special physical examination. All they could find was low blood pressure, so they concluded that it was dangerously low, and he was removed from active duty. Others more correctly have assessed what he called "split-second aggressiveness" as situational awareness. He was one of those people I'd not want to come up against.

It has bothered me that he was wounded while flanking a machine gun at Blanc Mont, when his job was runner. As time went on, I came to regard the 80th as an ill-fated company. The company had some outstanding leaders—Overton, Green, maybe even Kilduff. But they never lasted. There is reason to believe that the 80th was poorly led at Blanc Mont. By then, Dad was an old pro. It was his fourth battle. If they were ill-led, and if you came upon a lieutenant of the 78th who had his head screwed on straight, why not take up with him? The 78th on that day may have been brilliantly led, as their accomplishments were remarkable. I am not surprised that Dad was with them.

The mental scars of World War I are still present. The French still refuse to allow the German flag to fly over German cemeteries on French soil. It is difficult for me to see this as being to the credit of the French. What is to their credit is Marshal Foch. The more I learned of him in preparation for the anniversary trip, the more I came to respect his vision and judgment. Pétain called for more troops following Ludendorff's July 15 attack near Reims. Foch rejected the request and instead sent Mangin on the attack at Soissons. And that attack is what opened the Allies' march to victory.

The mental scars of World War II also are still present. I have traced the hail dancer's last flight from Tinian to Minami Tori Shima. And I have certainly thought about seeing those places. But the sky leaves few tracks. I could go to a place where the plane was hit, where it soared as bombs spilled out of the bay, and where the smoke from the burning tokyo tank in the portside forward bomb bay could be seen. I can come within a nautical mile of that place where the port wing touched the water and the cartwheeling began. I can go to a point which places me in the sea within a kilometer of where the broken PB4Y1 lies three thousand feet below the surface. But why? He has stayed close at hand for the last fifty years.

And finally, did the hail dancer have a name? Of course he did. It was Carl Andrew Brannen, Jr.

J. P. Brannen's Scrapbook

Bulldog fountain at Belleau, 1993. It is said that this is where the marines got their bulldog mascot motif. The Germans named the marines "Teufelhund," literally, "Devil dog."

Carl Brannen's World War I dog tags.

The Lion Fountain at Bouresches, 1992. The well was behind this wall.

Chauchat, *top,* and Hotchkiss at the Marine Corps Museum, Quantico, 1992.

The sunken road where Brannen was pinned by a machine gunner located in the copse, center of photo. The sugar beet mill was at the crossroads that borders the plowed field. The Cates' trench was to the right off the edge of this picture. Behind the copse is the Soissons–Château-Thierry highway. 1993.

Ruins of sugar beet mill at Villemontoire. The cobblestones and the embedded iron rails are all that is left. In the background is the small building housing the guest book and chapel for the British cemetery. 1993.

Undeveloped road mentioned in Major William's orders. Williams, oblivious to the enemy, led his battalion toward Bois de la Montagne in a column with the 80th Company up front. The column turned off the main road to follow a ravine, and the forest erupted with machine-gun fire. 1993.

Clearing at Kilduff ambush site, 1993.

Location of Germans that Scatterbrain found. They disappeared over the ridge to the right. 1993.

Capt. David R. Kilduff's marker in the U.S. cemetery near Thiaucourt, 1992.

Hindenberg line bunker northeast of Kilduff ambush site, 1993.

View from Essen trench toward Hill 210 west, at Blanc Mont taken from approximate position of 78th at beginning of advance. Note the exposure of the open terrain and the military exclusion area antennas on the horizon, 1995.

Road atop Blanc Mont along which the 2nd Battalion lined up after taking the ridge, 1993.

German dugout northside of the church at Sommepy. It was used as an aid station by the French before the Americans arrived and was likely so employed by the 2nd Division. It is probably the site where Brannen's wound was examined. 1993.

Street scene of the village of Les Isolettes where Brannen rejoined the 6th Regiment on October 25, 1918. 1995.

Meuse just north of the lock where the attempts to place footbridges failed on the night of November 10, 1918. 1995.

Site where Brannen crossed the Rhine with Horace Cooper at Bad Hönnigen as advanced Guard. 1993.

German soldier memorial to their World War I casualties, 1993.

Carl A. Brannen, Jr., at Texas A&M University, 1942.

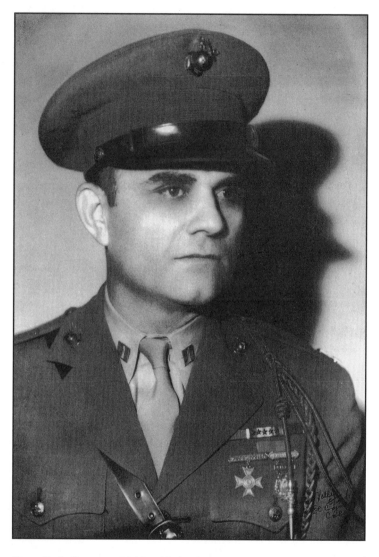

Capt. C. A. Brannen, 1943, with five battle stars on his victory medal.

Chapter 1: Parris Island, Crossing, Training

1. Jack Shulimson, "The First to Fight: Marine Corps Expansion 1914–1918," *Prologue* (Spring 1976): 5–16, reprinted in *Marine Corps Gazette*, Nov. 1988.

2. Russell F. Wiegley, *The American Way of War: A History of U.S. Military Strategy and Policy* (New York: Macmillan, 1973): 354.

3. In addition to Shulimson, see Rolfe L. Hillman, "Second to None: The Indianheads," *U.S. Naval Institute Proceedings* 103, no. 11 (Nov. 1987): 57–62.

4. Brannen describes his motivation for going to war in a simple but touching sentence: "I felt my family should do their bit in uniform and my age designated me as the most appropriate one." Marine Commandant Barnett would have been pleased to know of Brannen's testimony that the "First to Fight" posters were appealing.

If C. A. Brannen had been in his junior or senior year and had carried some star status in athletics, he might have been recruited to enter directly into Marine Corps officer training. In Henry Berry, *Make the Kaiser Dance* (New York: Arbor House, 1978), a lively book of 1976 interviews with World War I veterans,

Samuel Meek, who would lead a platoon in 82nd Company, recalls that in late April 1917, the marines sent an officer to the dean at Yale:

> *If Yale would furnish him a list of ten men with leadership qualifications, the Corps would immediately send them down to . . . Quantico for officers' training. The dean gave him my name. I was managing editor of the* Yale News. *Johnny Overton, the track captain; Bill LeGore, the baseball and football star; Bill Wallace, wrestling captain; Stan Burke, head of dramatics—people like that. We all accepted, and just like that, the Marines had ten new second lieutenants. (p. 88)*

Brannen, however, had no such opportunity and went the route of a marine rifleman, survived it all, and emerged as Private Brannen. It is tempting to speculate what would have happened if, a year or two older, he had been commissioned. He could have become a Marine Corps commandant or been killed leading a charge at Soissons.

5. Maj. Edward N. McClellan, who remains preeminent among those who wrote Marine Corps history as it happened, states in *The United States Marines in the World War,* rev. ed. (Washington, D.C.: Headquarters, U.S. Marine Corps, 1968): 21, that Parris Island trained 46,202 recruits for at least eight weeks, while another 11,901 were trained at Mare Island, Calif. Many, before shipping overseas, received advanced training at Quantico, Va. McClellan concludes: "The preliminary training received at the recruit depots was such that it fit the men for general service throughout the Marine Corps and resulted in men being well disciplined."

The Marine Corps, relatively small in numbers and under tight centralized control, did a better job of training front-line soldiers than did the army, in which new soldiers were trained within huge divisions as they were formed in scattered locations. In Laurence Stallings' anecdotal *The Doughboys: The Story of the AEF, 1917–1918* (New York: Harper and Row, 1963), Pvt. Leo Bailey, an early arrival in the army's 9th Infantry, reports that none in his company had fired a Springfield rifle, and a few had never fired a firearm of any kind (p. 37). Timothy K. Nenninger states that the necessity to speed army troops for the AEF buildup in France resulted in the employment of many untrained replacements: "In late September 1918, the 77th Division received 2,100 replacements. Over half lacked rudimentary infantry skills. Many had not been issued weapons prior to reporting to the division and did not know how to care for or use a rifle. The day after receiving these replacements, the division jumped off at daylight as part of the Meuse-Argonne attack" (Stallings, *Doughboys,* 149). See also Edward M. Coffman, *The War to End All Wars* (Madison: University of Wisconsin Press, 1986): 64–68; and Stephen Lofgren, "Unready for War: The U.S. Army in World War One," *Army History* 22 (Spring 1992): 11–19.

    6. "Muster Roll of the 80th Company," *Muster Roll of the U.S. Marine Corps,* (U.S. Marine Corps, Marine Corps Historical Center, Research Section, Navy Yard, Washington, D.C., June 1918): microfilm. This records no Sergeant Boynton, but lists Sgt. Richard Boydston as serving in Company H aboard Parris Island. I find no record of either Sergeant Boynton's or Sergeant Boydston's being killed in action in France.

    7. The AP-1 transport USS *Henderson,* named for a Marine Corps lieutenant who served aboard the famed USS *Constitution* in 1812 and held the post of commandant for thirty-eight years, deserves a separate tribute for her fundamental support of Marine Corps operations. Launched in Philadelphia in June 1916, with space for 1,500 men and twenty-four mules, she made her initial trip to France with the first-to-ship 5th Marines on June 14, 1917, just over two months after war had been declared. Before the Armistice in November 1918, *Henderson* made eight more deliveries of men and supplies. She concluded World War I service by making another eight trips to return an estimated ten thousand veterans. *Henderson* then served as a troop rotation ship in the Caribbean, carrying marines and their dependents to Cuba, Haiti, and other islands. After extensive repairs, she continued carrying navy and marine personnel, with several glimpses of history in the making. She carried President Warren Harding on an inspection trip to Alaska, and he reviewed the fleet off Seattle from the deck of the *Henderson* on July 27, 1923. Five days later, Harding was dead of a sudden, mysterious illness. In May 1927, the *Henderson* carried marines to Shanghai and remained in China for six months, while her crew helped protect American nationals from warring factions. Until 1941, she ran regularly from San Francisco to stations in the Philippines and other Pacific islands. When World War II arrived, she made twenty voyages to Hawaii and on her last trip took nurses to Noumea and Seabees to the Solomon Islands, re-

turning to San Francisco in September 1943. Rebuilt as the hospital ship USS *Bountiful,* she continued to serve the Marine Corps, evacuating casualties from, among many other places, epic actions at Peleliu and Iwo Jima. A second *Henderson,* the destroyer DD-785, was launched in May 1945. James L. Mooney, ed., *Dictionary of American Naval Fighting Ships,* rev. ed. (Washington, D.C.: U.S. Navy, 1977): 3:295–96.

8. Brannen's mention of "big naval guns" surely refers to the expedited program to produce special railway carriages to allow the use of five U.S. Navy 14-inch naval guns on French battlefields. Between September 6 and November 1, 1918, the guns fired 782 rounds at ranges up to twenty-two miles. Brig. Gen. E. R. Lewis, for his article, "The 14-Inch Naval Railway Batteries," *Naval History* 5, no. 1 (Spring 1991): 41–45, prepared annotations of comprehensive photographs of this episode. It is questionable, however, whether crews for these guns were a-board *Henderson* with Brannen. U.S. Navy, *The United States Naval Railway Batteries in France* (Washington, D.C.: Naval Historical Center, 1988), states that the first contingent—250 men and eight officers—arrived in St. Nazaire on June 10, and the second contingent of 207 men and six officers arrived on June 29. By June 8, Brannen already had joined the 80th Company at Belleau Wood.

9. Brannen stated earlier that he got to Brest "the first part of May" and within a week had taken his first long train ride. We can by deduction trace his route. The formation and initial training of the 2nd Division took place in the Bourmont area in eastern France, directly south of St. Mihiel, southwest of Nancy, and just east of AEF general headquarters at Chaumont. For its second phase of training, mid-March to mid-May, the division was moved to Sector Toulon in the Verdun area near the north end of the St. Mihiel salient. There, battalions were rotated in and out of a French division's trench positions. The first division casualty occurred on April 1, a man killed by German artillery on a reserve position; and in mid-April a company of the 6th Marines received a massive German gas attack that killed forty one. Brannen's replacement battalion apparently went first to this location, but his stay here was short. Oliver L. Spaulding and John W. Wright, *The Second Division American Expeditionary Force in France, 1917–1919* (New York: Hillman Press, 1937; reprint, Nashville, Tenn.: Battery Press, 1989): 13–28; Alan R. Millett, *Semper Fidelis: The His-*

tory of the United States Marine Corps (New York: Macmillan, 1980): 297–301.

10. Brannen was assigned a weapon that has earned a place in military history as "probably one of the crudest, most unreliable and cheaply made guns ever to come into service." Further, "no more crudely designed or ugly automatic weapon has ever been put into the hands of any first-rate power." French *poilus* alleged that it was put together from battlefield scraps, while the doughboys claimed it was assembled from sardine cans. Designed to supplement an adequate heavy machine gun, this nineteen-pound light machine gun with its half-moon magazine attached below the barrel was officially designated the *Fusil Mitrailler Modele* 1915, CSRG. The last letters represented the names of the accepting committee, the first being one Mr. Chauchat. Brannen recalled it as the "French Chau Chau." Other Americas called it the Sho-Sho or anything remotely connected phonetically with Chauchat. The Americans purchased almost sixteen thousand of the 8mm version and contracted for nineteen thousand more with U.S. caliber 30-06. The guns were issued one per twelve-man squad, with two men designated as ammunition carriers, each man carrying four hundred rounds in the twenty-round magazine. W. H. B. Smith, *Small Arms of the World*, 10th ed., rev. Joseph E. Smith (Harrisburg, Pa.: Stackpole Co., 1973): 132–33.

11. In the next chapter, he is moving inexorably toward first-hand experience of war.

Chapter 2: Belleau Wood

1. Spaulding and Wright, *Second Division AEF in France*, 1–5.

2. S. L. A. Marshall, *The American Heritage History of World War I* (New York: American Heritage Publishing Co., 1964), 281.

3. James G. Harbord, *The American Army in France, 1917–1918* (Boston: Little, Brown, 1936), 262–63. The best account of Pershing's relationships with his general officers in the AEF is Donald Smythe, *Pershing: General of the Armies* (Bloomington: Indiana University Press, 1986). See also Alan R. Millett, *The General: Robert L. Bullard and the Officership of the United States Army, 1881–1925* (Westport, Conn.: Greenwood Press, 1975).

4. Shulimson, "First to Fight," passim.

5. By far the best study of the campaign is Robert Asprey, *At Belleau Wood* (New York: G. P. Putnam's Sons, 1965). See also

Millett, *Semper Fidelis*, 301–18. For a German perspective, see Lt. Col. Ernst Otto, "The Battles for the Possession of Belleau Woods, June 1918," *U.S. Naval Institute Proceedings* 54, no. 11 (Nov. 1928): 941–62.

6. Asprey, *At Belleau Wood*, 182–86.

7. J. Robert Moskin, *The U.S. Marine Corps Story* (New York: McGraw-Hill, 1982), 102.

8. Brig. Gen. Edwin H. Simmons, *The United States Marines: The First Two Hundred Years, 1775–1976* (New York: Viking Press, 1974), 136, 227. Gibbons' own account is in Floyd Gibbons, *And They Thought We Wouldn't Fight* (New York: George H. Doran Co., 1918), 283–322. See also Asprey, *At Belleau Wood*, 167–77; Moskin, *U.S. Marine Corps Story*, 102.

9. In this case and in others, Vandoren's dates and casualty figures do not tally with the company's muster roll. On the roll of the 80th Company for June 1918 it appears that a casualty was recorded as of the date the man was evacuated from the battle area, rather than the date on which he was wounded or killed. *Muster Roll of the U.S. Marine Corps*, microfilm.

10. The 2nd Division's 3rd Brigade consisted of the army's 9th and 23rd Infantry regiments. The Marine brigade, commanded by the army's Brig. Gen. James G. Harbord since May 5, consisted of the 5th and 6th Marine Regiments and the 6th Machine Gun Battalion. Harbord was promoted to major general and moved up to command the entire division on July 15. Hillman, "Second to None," 57–62.

11. Brannen has omitted mention of the division's movement from Sector Toulon to Chaumont-en-Vixen, conducted beginning May 15. Taken out of its training phase and repositioned for quick insertion into active combat to meet the crisis, the division moved by a long rail movement to Chaumont-en-Vixen, which is northeast of Paris, midway to Amiens. From there, the division began its move to Château-Thierry–Belleau on Sunday, May 30. It is probable that Brannen moved, still as part of a replacement battalion, "sometime after the first of June." The text, however, leaves open the possibility that the replacement battalion did not go to Chaumont-en-Vixen, but instead went, by a train trip that lasted a full day and night, direct to St. Denis and Meaux, where a truck movement began. Spaulding and Wright, *Second Division AEF in France*, 13–37.

12. This catchy phrase, "Retreat, hell!" is attributed to many

persons, including an army colonel of artillery. A recent and authoritative source, Simmons, *United States Marines,* 110, attributes it to a shout by the commander of the 5th Marines, Col. Wendell "Whispering Buck" Neville. Brannen's account mixes in a bit of the story that, when the brigade commander, Harbord, was told by the French to dig some contingency trenches to the rear, he replied, "We will dig no trenches to fall back to. The Marines will hold where they stand." Harbord, cited in Smythe, *Pershing,* 138; Millett, *Semper Fidelis,* 493. George Clark, *Retreat, Hell! We Just Got Here* (Pike, N.H.: Brass Hat, n.d.), 11, attributes it to Capt. Lloyd Williams of the 51st Company or possibly to Williams' battalion commander, Maj. Frederic Wise.

13. Brannen still was with the replacement battalion when he saw wounded being evacuated on the day after June 6.

14. Brannen now was at the business end of the personnel replacement pipeline and had arrived at his combat unit, the 80th Company of the 6th Marine Regiment. He did not know it yet, but he was there for the duration. The Muster Roll of the 80th Company for June 1918, shows that on June 8, Carl A. Brannen, Marine Corps Reserve Class 4, was one of thirty-eight men assigned from 138th Company of the 2nd Replacement Battalion. Other replacement contingents arrived throughout the month. *Muster Roll of the U.S. Marine Corps,* microfilm.

Here an explanation of the World War I designation of Marine Corps units is necessary. In an army regiment, the designation of companies—the basic fighting element of 250 men—was a neat alphabetical arrangement within any numbered regiment:

1st Battalion: Companies A, B, C, D
2nd Battalion: Companies E, F, G, H
3rd Battalion: Companies I, K, L, M

The marines brought with them a traditional system of random numbering of companies, the present example of which is Brannen's assignment to 80th Company. Since that time, it has been necessary for students of the history of the 2nd Division to keep at hand the "conversion chart" in McClellan, *United States Marines in the World War,* 29. Thus, his 80th Company translates to Company G, 2nd Battalion, 6th Marines.

15. Capt. Bailey M. Coffenberg, who had commanded the company since Mar. 12, in fact was not wounded to an extent requiring evacuation but on June 17 was moved to the position of battalion quartermaster. He was then, as Brannen states, replaced by

Capt. Egbert T. Lloyd, who had commanded Brannen's replacement company. *Muster Roll of the U.S. Marine Corps,* microfilm.

16. Brannen was made to jump in fright when, right behind him, "one of the new men shot the trigger finger off his right hand." This can be nothing other than a wound self-inflicted to avoid combat, since it would be physically impossible to do it accidentally. Later in the war, the AEF faced, and recorded in official reports, a major problem in the thousands of "stragglers" from combat divisions who drifted to the rear on whatever pretext and remained in those safer areas. If self-inflicted wounds were numerous, they seldom are mentioned in the literature.

17. Brannen's stay in foxholes for "a few days" reflects the fact that his 2nd Battalion was assigned no major attack missions until June 13. Asprey writes, "Since its relief from the line Bouresches-Triangle, Holcomb's tired battalion had been resting while sorting out its units and gear and working replacements [such as Brannen and friends] into the companies." On June 12, the calm was disrupted by German shelling. During the night, Holcomb received a message from Brigade Commander Harbord that the Germans were mounting a counterattack on Belleau Wood; Holcomb must, by 3:50 A.M., reposition his companies to a support position in the wood northeast of Lucy-le-Bocage. The companies, including Brannen's 80th, were turned out for a forced night march to the new area, there to await orders for disposition. On the afternoon of June 13, Holcomb was ordered to move his battalion to relieve Maj. Frederic Wise's 2nd Battalion, 5th Marines, exhausted by days of combat within the wood. Disrupted from the outset by a massive German bombardment of high explosives and mustard gas, Holcomb arrived at Wise's position about 3 A.M. with less than two of his four companies. Within the next two hours, some 150 men from the other companies were gathered in. Even after the march, as the gas continued its deadly work on contaminated men, all of 96th Company and most of 78th Company were evacuated as casualties. Asprey, *At Belleau Wood,* 276–79. In the June Muster Roll of 96th Company, seven pages of entries trace the disposition of these men. There is personal and collective drama tucked away in the musty archives: some died, some left permanently through medical channels, some returned to the company for duty. *Muster Roll of the U.S. Marine Corps,* microfilm.

18. The attack on Bouresches initially was led by Company

Comdr. Donald F. Duncan, who, as noted above, was killed, leaving Lt. James F. Robertson and Lt. Clifton Cates to carry on. Robertson returned to get reinforcements, so Cates was the only officer in Bouresches. Lt. Fielding Robinson at this time was an aide-de-camp to Brig. Gen. James Harbord. *Muster Roll of the U.S. Marine Corps,* microfilm; Asprey, *At Belleau Wood,* 182–84.

19. "Get your head down, Greeny." Brannen, the new man, still had on his green marine uniform. Thomason explains: "For the 5th and 6th Marines had long since worn out their forest-green Marine uniforms and were wearing Army khaki, while the replacements came in new green clothing." John W. Thomason, *Fix Bayonets!* (Washington, D.C.: Marine Corps Association, 1925), 45.

20. This night march is the occasion upon which Holcomb's battalion was called forward on June 12, to react to a possible German counterattack on Belleau Wood. In 1919, 1st Lt. Lucien H. Vandoren wrote in "A Brief History of the Second Battalion, Sixth Regiment, U.S. Marine Corps," Clifton B. Cates Papers, Marine Corps Historical Center, Navy Yard, Washington, D.C.: "We were ordered from Corps reserve to proceed to Bouresches to counterattack and retake the village . . . but before we got there orders were received that the village was safe and we were moved to a wood [near Lucy-le-Bocage] to await darkness before moving again." George C. MacGillivray and George Clark, *A History of the 80th Company, Sixth Marines* (Pike, N.H.: Brass Hat, n.d.), 4. Thus began the battalion's disastrous move to relieve Wise's battalion in Belleau Wood, and the mass gas casualties in 78th and 96th companies.

21. The muster roll indicates that this was probably Wesley G. Bedker, who had made the replacement trip with Brannen and was also assigned on June 8. *Muster Roll of the U.S. Marine Corps,* microfilm.

22. Lieutenant Cates apparently stayed with 80th Company while new personnel became available to reconstitute his 96th Company. He is carried on the muster roll of the 96th as commanding the former company June 6–20. *Muster Roll of the U.S. Marine Corps,* microfilm. This marked the beginning of Brannen's long-lived admiration for Cates. Brannen, in his final chapter, tells of being selected for Captain Cates' company in the AEF's Composite Regiment Honor Guard that, in 1919, made many ceremonial representations. Brannen's daughter, Frances B. Vick, recalls that her father maintained correspondence with Cates through the

1960s. The only correspondence found follows. This letter from Gen. C. B. Cates, Nov. 22, 1968, The Landing, Edgewater, Maryland, to C. A. Brannen:

Dear Brannen:

My apology for not answering your letters long before this, but old father time has slowed me down and my correspondence has suffered.

Your letter brought back may fond memories . . . of the Composit Regiment—there will never be another like it.

A few days ago, I mailed you a copy of our 96th Company History, which may have something of interest to you. Although it is mostly about our Company, a lot of it applys to the 80th Company as well.

You probably do not remember it, but I served with your Company for about ten days in Belleau Woods after ours had been wiped out by gas. Capt. Coffenberg—I think—was the company commander.

If you should get up this way I would be most pleased to see you and refight our battles and our parades in Paris, London, New York and Washington.

My very, very best to you and yours, as ever,

C. B. Cates

A note from Mrs. C. B. Cates on June 30, 1970 written on a card "The family of General Clifton Bledsoe Cates acknowledges with deep gratitude your kind expression of sympathy," reads in part:

Dear Mr. Brannen:

Clifton was optimistic about the future until a week or two before he died. World War One was always his first interest and anything or anyone connected with those days meant much to him. General Pershing's Honor Guard and that Great Parade was one of his highlights!

Clifton never willfully let anyone down, but he was very, very sick. [Apparently C. A. Brannen wrote Cates for a photograph, not realizing how sick Cates was, read of his death and wrote a letter of sympathy to the family.] *I will find a picture for you eventually. I do appreciate your letter.*

Sincerely,

Jane M. Cates

If a photograph was received, the Brannen family has not located it. Brannen is not indexed in the Cates correspondence held at the Marine Corps Historical Center, Navy Yard, Washington, D.C.

23. Lt. John W. Overton came to duty with 80th Company on June 17. He was one of ten Yale students listed by Samuel Meek as having been recruited for officer training because of their leadership qualifications. Berry, *Make the Kaiser Dance*, 88. Brannen's platoon leader, John W. Overton, should not be confused with Capt. Macon C. Overton, who commanded 76th Company (Company C, 1st Battalion, 6th Marines).

24. It is likely that Brannen transposed an incident from the July battle at Soissons back to this time. "Sergeant Willie" is probably Sgt. Edward L. Wilkinson, who came to the company on June 11. The Muster Roll of the 80th Company for July shows that this Sergeant Wilkinson was wounded and evacuated on July 19, the one day that the 6th Marines were in combat at Soissons. The "fellow named Walker" who volunteered with Brannen probably is Pvt. Henry C. Walker, who does not appear on the Muster Roll of the 80th Company until July. *Muster Roll of the U.S. Marine Corps*, microfilm.

Brannen should have been given a high award for bravery here. The records of awards in this war are sprinkled liberally with Distinguished Service Crosses awarded to soldiers who volunteered to recover wounded comrades in exposed areas. Such an award would have depended on the circumstances and, to a large extent, on who in the upward chain of command had the time and initiative to write up a proper recommendation.

25. By June 17, at the insistence of the division commander, Maj. Gen. Omar Bundy, a battalion from the 7th Infantry Regiment of the adjacent U.S. 3rd Division was made available to relieve Sibley's 3rd Battalion and Holcomb's 2nd Battalion of the 6th Marines. Despite the series of violent actions in the early weeks, the June muster roll for Brannen's 80th Company shows totals of only twenty-two killed and sixty-three wounded. *Muster Roll of the U.S. Marine Corps*, microfilm.

On the morning of June 26, Belleau Wood was finally cleared of Germans. The 2nd Division lost 170 officers and 8,793 men; of these, 112 officers and 4,598 men were marines of the 4th Brigade. The action of American troops in the course of securing the insignificant terrain at Belleau Wood is a famous episode of American military history. It seemed to prove to impatient and cynical Allies that American soldiers would fight. The Germans themselves created their own "test case" by issuing the following announcement to troops opposing the Americans:

> *Should the Americans at our front even temporarily gain the upper hand, it would have a most unfavorable effect for us as regards the morale of the Allies and the duration of the war. In the fighting that now confronts us, we are not concerned about the occupation or non-occupation of this or that unimportant wood or village, but rather with the question as to whether Anglo-American propaganda, that the American Army is equal to or even superior to the Germans, will be successful. (Unnumbered order by the German 28th Division, dated June 8, cited in U.S., American Battlefield Monuments Commission, 2nd Division, Summary of Operations, 15)*

26. The Aisne-Marne cemetery near Belleau Wood is pictured and described in one of the most useful books ever compiled on the American experience in France: U.S., American Battlefield Monuments Commission, *American Armies and Battlefields in Europe* (Washington, D.C.: U.S. Government Printing Office, 1938; reprinted for U.S. Army, Center of Military History, Washington, D.C., 1992), 51–54. The maps are superb and comprehensive. This cemetery, laid out in a sweeping curve at the foot of the hill upon which stands Belleau Wood, contains 2,288 graves. The majority of those buried here are from the units which fought in the immediate vicinity.

27. MacGillivray and Clark, *History of the 80th Company*, 4, states that twenty men of 80th Company, "with a like number from each company of the division, were sent to Paris for this parade."

Chapter 3: Soissons

1. For general accounts of the 2nd Division at Soissons, see Spaulding and Wright, *Second Division AEF in France*, 96–132. For the Marine brigade, see Edwin N. McClellan, "The Aisne-Marne Offensive," 2 pts., *Marine Corps Gazette* 6, no. 1 (Mar. 1921): 66–84, and no. 2 (June 1921): 188–227; Brig. Gen. Robert H. Williams, "The 4th Marine Brigade: Soissons," *Marine Corps Gazette* 64, no. 12 (Dec. 1980): 59–64; and Brig. Gen. E. H.

Simmons, "The First Day at Soissons," *Fortitudine* (Summer 1993): 3–11, and "The Second Day at Soissons," in *Fortitudine* (Fall 1993): 3–10.

2. For a biographical sketch of Mangin, see Alistar Horne, *The Price of Glory* (New York: Penguin Books, 1981), 228–30.

3. Mangin's operations in July are summarized in Spaulding and Wright, *Second Division AEF in France*, 97; and more critically in Stallings, *Doughboys*, 142–43.

4. James G. Harbord, *Leaves from a War Diary* (New York: Dodd, Mead, 1925), 318–19.

5. John J. Pershing, *My Experiences in the World War*, 2 vols. (New York: Frederick A. Stokes Co., 1931), 2:163–64.

6. Denig's letter is in Kemper F. Cowling, *Dear Folks at Home*— (Boston: Houghton Mifflin, 1919), 250–59. See also Robert Denig, "Diary of a Marine Officer During the World War," Marine Corps Personal Paper Collection, Marine Corps Historical Center, Navy Yard, Washington, D.C.

7. At this point, Brannen begins to use "we" to indicate everybody up to the entire Marine brigade. The 5th Marines indeed went into battle without slowing up and with their supporting weapons and supplies left far behind. But Brannen's 6th Marines were held in corps reserve for this first day and were, at daybreak, floundering in the mud of the forest, moving up behind the 5th Marines. Incidentally, Brannen joins many other late-arriving Americans in inaccurately appropriating the phrase "over the top"— inaccurately, because the term is a carry-over from the years of trench warfare, when countless thousands of soldiers, on a whistled or shouted signal from their leader, climbed up a fire step and leaped over the top of the parapet of a revetted trench. The usage later was shortened so that "we went over" meant the start of any specific attack. The Americans did not begin any advances from prepared trenches at this battle, and they seldom did so in later battles.

8. Mangin fully expected that his Cavalry Corps would be able to exploit a breakthrough and wreak havoc in the German rear, but that never happened. The cavalry was forever lurking in the rear with banners waving; getting in the way of foot troops; and, from time to time, making abortive forays that were destroyed by artillery or machine-gun fire.

9. On the morning of July 18, the 2nd Division placed three attacking regiments in the front lines, left to right (north to south):

the 5th Marines, the 9th Infantry, and the 23rd Infantry. Col. Harry Lee's 6th Marines were held to exploit any successful breakthrough. By the end of the day, the division had moved well ahead of its adjacent unit to the north, the French 1st Moroccan Division, and that division, in turn, had exceeded the advance of the American 1st Division on the northern axis.

The morning attack of the 5th Marines was swift but immediately became a scattering of units that fought forward on their own momentum. The marines, with the 9th and 23rd Infantry, attained a general line in advance of Vierzy ravine. A second attack in the late afternoon was delayed by near-total breakdown of command and control; in final result, elements of the 5th Marines supplemented the 23rd Infantry in clearing the town of Vierzy. The distance gained was about five miles. Those front lines were manned by exhausted soldiers without food and water; in every corner of the arena, day's end found soldiers neglected from lack of adequate medical support. Spaulding and Wright, *Second Division AEF in France,* 116–26.

10. Division Commander Harbord, having at 2 A.M. received from a French staff officer an order for continuation of the attack at 4 A.M. on July 19, could under these circumstances only commit the 6th Marines, reinforced with a battalion from the division's engineer regiment. They were to continue the attack to control the German's lifeline in this salient, the Soissons–Château-Thierry road.

The 6th did not get under way until 6:30 A.M. It moved toward the front lines. During the night, the Germans had pulled up every possible bit of reinforcement, and those worn, desperate forces knew that an American attack could be expected in the morning. The marines were to attack over the perfectly flat terrain.

The regiment deployed with Holcomb's 2nd Battalion on the left, Hughes' 1st Battalion on the right, and Sibley's 3rd Battalion in support. The essence of the stark official record of the action of Holcomb's battalion is quickly stated:

> *The zero hour was 0820 and we were supported by tanks. The advance to our front lines (held by 9th and 23rd Infantry) a kilometer distant, was across perfectly open wheat fields. Our pace, because of the necessity of following the tanks, was slow, and the advance over the entire distance was through a heavy barrage put down by the enemy. When we passed through our*

front lines his machine guns proved most troublesome. We were halted after a gain of about one kilometer because we had nothing left with which to continue the attack. (Vandoren, "Brief History of the Second Battalion.")

11. The Muster Roll of the 80th Company, July 1918, shows that Pvt. Forest Williams died of wounds on July 19. *Muster Roll of the U.S. Marines,* microfilm.

12. Muster Roll of the 80th Company, July 1918, shows Gunnery Sgt. John Shrank had joined 80th Company as a replacement on July 13. He had six days in a strange new world, then about an hour of the war to end all wars. Behind each of these muster roll entries is the history of a young man. *Muster Roll of the U.S. Marines,* microfilm.

13. Brannen tells of bandaging one of the nearby wounded, then writes a very perceptive sentence: "They both left for the rear, hoping to make the hospital." Several "walking wounded" from other units in the division wrote of how they planned, in lucid moments, how they could get off the battlefield, under their own power, before being killed. A real concern was that, if a man started walking back through the wheat field and fell, unable to continue, he would suffer, unobserved, a slow death from his wounds.

14. Here begin Brannen's personal remembrances of the neglect of those dead and dying on the Soissons battlefield. It was becoming apparent that something was terribly amiss in the medical support for front-line troops. The developing situation is evident in a message sent at 6:40 P.M. from Col. Harry Lee, commanding the 6th Marines, to Marine Brigade Comdr. Wendell Neville, reporting that it was still impossible to move between positions without drawing deadly fire. Lee's battalion commanders—Hughes, Holcomb, Sibley—had reported losses at from 40 to 50 percent. The message continued with a poignant passage still wrenching to read these many years later: "[The battalion commanders'] appeals for doctors, ambulances and stretcher bearers are pathetic. Cannot the ammunition [be] used to evacuate the two hundred or more cases now [at the regimental aid station] under Doctor Boone? Some may be saved by prompt removal." U.S. Army, *Records of the 2nd Division (Regular),* vol. 5: *Field Messages* (Washington, D.C.: Army War College, 1927).

15. Lieutenant Cates at this time sent a message back which became important in Marine history: "I have only 2 men left out of my company and 20 of other companies. We need support, but it is almost suicidal to try to get it here as we are swept by machine gun fire and a constant artillery barrage is on us. I have no one on my left and very few on my right. I will hold." Quoted in Robert H. Williams, "4th Marine Brigade: Soissons," 64.

16. By early afternoon it was clear to Division Commander Harbord that he could expect no more of these troops. He ordered them to hold in place and dispatched to Berdoulat, commanding French XX Corps, a full-page letter reviewing the circumstances of the morning attack, describing the present situation, and requesting relief. He asked that "further prosecution of the offensive in our front be done by divisions in the second line, passing them through our present position." The elements of the division were brought out in the dark hours of that night and on the following morning. Spaulding and Wright, *Second Division AEF in France,* 129.

17. Muster Roll of the 80th Company, July 1918, shows the man Brannen helped carry out was Pvt. Horace J. Cooper, who had arrived in Brannen's own group of replacements to join 80th Company on June 8. *Muster Roll of the U.S. Marine Corps,* microfilm.

18. "Slum gullion" often tasted as bad as it sounds. It was an expedient beef stew made of too little beef and whatever else the cooks could scrounge. Berry, *Make the Kaiser Dance,* 283.

19. By the end of the war, the French were making full use of their colonial troops—those from north of the Sahara, such as Moroccans, and those from south of the Sahara, such as Senegalese. In this paragraph, Brannen is passing along the fearsome reputation of the Senegalese, who, during the main attack at Soissons, formed part of the French 1st Moroccan Division, and who, on July 18, sometimes were intermingled with elements of the 5th Marines. It would be fair to say that the Senegalese were intensely feared by the Germans, who protested that it was inhuman to use black troops against white ones; they were a concern to the French, too, because they sometimes fought their own impromptu battles. Americans were both wary and fascinated.

20. Brannen is not exaggerating the final tragedy in the experience of the 6th Marines on the Soissons battlefield. A battalion surgeon wrote, "Few spots in history, in degree of suffering, wasted

life, and helplessness of medical personnel to give aid equal that which occurred in connection with this cave during the night and morning of 19–20 July 1918." He was referring to the 6th Marines regimental aid station, established in one of the large caves near Vierzy, which provided protection for some two thousand casualties who had been collected there during the day and night of July 19: "From this point to the nearest ambulance pool . . . the distance was about 15 kilometers. Because of French military orders prohibiting the use of roads by ambulances (thus giving a strict priority to ammunition and supply trucks), this station was forced to carry on its work without dressings, water, food, litters, morphine, or any other form of medical supplies. Hundreds of walking wounded and many others ordinarily considered litter cases were passed by this station because of this condition. Every effort to have the order rescinded failed and as great as was the contingency."

To understand this crisis in medical support, we must consider what was planned to be available and what in fact was on hand. The marines, having no medical element of their own, were supported by a Navy Medical Department detachment tailored for this expedition to France. Each regiment was supported by seven medical officers, three dental surgeons, and forty-eight medical corpsmen. From this total came battalion aid stations and, for the rifle companies, two to four corpsmen.

In the 2nd Division's logistics units, collectively labeled "Trains," the 2nd Sanitary Train, at a strength of fifty officers and nine hundred men, provided four ambulance companies and four field hospitals. The army corps, the next echelon above division, held three ambulance companies and three field hospitals. The breakdown came from several causes. First and most readily invoked, there was no upward chain of American resources and responsibility beyond division level. Although technically under administrative control of the newly formed American III Corps, which was formed too late to serve as a tactical control headquarters under Mangin's Tenth Army, the American 1st and 2nd Divisions were in full measure under French control. Next, while not detailed here, the division's medical resources had been drastically drained by the unexpectedly high level of casualties to the 5th Marines and the two army regiments on the day before. Next, as noted above, the French imposed battlefield regulations, based on their own harsh experience, which assigned medical vehicles a lower priority. Major Lay, the regiment's adjutant, added the following note to Lee's 6:40 P.M. message cited above: "Ambulances are blocked in the jam on the roads. It takes three hours to go distances which before took one-half hour. They can only make one trip a day on that account. I have sent runners and messages to Division Headquarters to get transportation for the wounded and will have ammunition trucks filled with wounded and sent to the rear. The shell fire and machine gun fire is so heavy that many trucks and ambulances have been hit and destroyed. Everything in God's name is being done to get the wounded out."

From the American point of view, responsibility lay directly with French Tenth Army, as they had not filled in for the absence of American support at corps and army level. Pershing was deeply disturbed at the reports, calling the situation "a damned poor piece of staff work." He demanded that all future French plans involving U.S. divisions give adequate advance warning, so that the Americans could set up their own hospitalization and evacuation facilities.

This section on medical support is compiled from George C. Strott, *The Medical Department of the United States Navy with the Army and Marine Corps in France in World War I* (Washington, D.C.: U.S. Navy, 1947), passim; Richard Derby, *Wade In, Sanitary!* (New York: G. P. Putnam's Sons, 1919), 90–96; Lt. Gen. Hunter Liggett, *A.E.F.: Ten Years Ago in France* (New York: Dodd, Mead, 1928), 319; Spaulding and Wright, *Second Division AEF in France,* 1; Smythe, *Pershing,* 156; and McClellan, "Aisne-Marne Offensive," 215–16. For the status of American III Corps, see Millett, *The General,* 382–83.

21. Vandoren, "Brief History of the Second Battalion," tells that less than two hundred of the four companies' men marched out, with Captain Lloyd, Lieutenant Shinkle, and Lieutenant Cates being the company officers not killed or wounded. MacGillivray and Clark, *History of the 80th Company,* compiled in 1919 by Lieutenant Vandoren, lists Lieutenants Overton and Roy as killed; Lieutenants Schneider, Taylor, and Erhart as wounded; four men killed, eighty-four wounded, and twelve missing in action (p. 4). From the best official source, I count 109 total casualties on the Muster Roll of the 80th Company for July 1918. *Muster Roll of the U.S. Marine Corps,* microfilm.

22. Note carefully Brannen's wording: "some fifteen or twenty men who claimed they got lost." The word *claimed* is loaded with

disdain. Even at this early stage of American participation, an element of our soldiery devised ways to get from the front to the rear and stay there. Some never crossed the line of departure, some feigned wounds, some took any opportunity to help a casualty to safety. (Recall Holcomb's instant order when a wounded man asked Sergeant Paradis for help: "Let the medics take care of him!") Messengers sent to the rear could not bring themselves to make the return trip. "The stragglers," they sometimes came back to their units after the battlefield became silent. The 2nd Division's attack order for July 18 provided that "the Commanding Officer, Military Police will establish a line of straggler posts," and subordinate units down to battalion included a similar provision. McClellan, "Aisne-Marne Offensive," 74. Coffman, *War to End All Wars*, 332–33, gives an estimate that, by the end of October, there were about a hundred thousand stragglers. When the 2nd Division's Col. Preston Brown, noted above as a tough, cranky cookie, was moved to command the 3rd Division, he authorized throwing bombs into dugouts if men refused to come out. Smythe, *Pershing*, 218–19.

23. On a road through the Forest of Retz, the French erected a statue of a lady in mourning veil, standing erect on a pedestal of marble with her back against a pillar. In one hand she holds a sword, in the other a laurel wreath, her arm half-extended as though to crown the victor. The French inscription translates as "Passing Stranger, Here Pause." Harbord, *AEF in France*, 338.

Chapter 4: St. Mihiel

1. Wiegley, *American Way of War*, 201.

2. Smythe, *Pershing*, 75.

3. Ibid., 179–80.

4. Ibid., 179–82.

5. U.S. Army, *Records of the 2nd Division (Regular)*, vol. 1, 6th Marines Field Order No. 1435, dated Sept. 11, 1918.

6. Spaulding and Wright, *Second Division AEF in France*, 153–55.

7. For official documentation of the fight on Sept. 15, see *History of the Sixth Regiment, United States Marines* (Tientsin, China: Tientsin Press, 1929): 30; and U.S. Army, *Records of the 2nd Division*, vol. 5, CO 1/6, Field Message to CO 6th Marines, 0050, Sept. 15, 1918. Williams' version is found in U.S. Army,

Records of the 2nd Division, vol. 7, CO 2/6, Report of Operations, Sept. 1–30, 1918. Second Lieutenant Adams' report is in U.S. Army, *Records of the 2nd Division,* vol. 7, CO, 78th Company, Report of Operations, Sept. 15, 1918. See also Don V. Paradis, "Memoirs of Don V. Paradis, Former Gunnery Sergeant, USMC," transcript of an oral history conducted on Sept. 17, 1973, Marine Corps Personal Paper Collection, Marine Corps Historical Center, Navy Yard, Washington, D.C. 116–19, 174. Graves B. Erskine's account as the battalion scout officer is in Erskine, interview by Brig. Gen. Bemis M. Frank, Oral History Collection, History and Museums Division, U.S. Marine Corps, Washington, D.C., 62–66. A pertinent German report is found in *Records of German Units Opposed to the 2nd Division,* vol. 6, CO 2/398th Infanterie Regiment, Report of Operations, Sept. 15, 1918.

8. The "word leaked out" from the rumor mill, in this case. Metz had been dropped as an objective of the 1st American Army. However, had Pershing pushed on for Metz, as advocated by officers such as Col. Douglas MacArthur of the 42nd Division, the casualties could have been enormous.

9. 1st Lt. David R. Kilduff, USMC, was awarded a Silver Star and promoted to captain posthumously for his actions at St. Mihiel. Kilduff was from Berkeley, Calif. He died of a gunshot wound to his right side on Sept. 15, 1918. MacGillivray and Clark, *History of the 80th Company,* ii; *Casualty List, American Expeditionary Forces,* (U.S. Marine Corps, Marine Corps Historical Center, Research Section, Navy Yard, Washington, D.C., n.d.): microfilm. USMC.

10. The Americans had entered the war using obsolete infantry tactics. Prewar doctrine had taught soldiers to pin down defenders with sustained, accurate rifle fire. According to U.S. Army, *Field Service Regulations, 1914, Corrected to Apr. 1917* (Washington, D.C.: U.S. War Department, 1917), riflemen were expected to build "fire superiority" over the enemy while other riflemen maneuvered forward. But even the superb marksmen of the Marine brigade had found it nearly impossible to overcome with rifle fire the devastating effects of well-emplaced machine guns. Infantry advances without artillery support were rare, and they were costly even by First World War standards. This was a primary cause of the four years of trench stalemate, and probably also the reason that the AEF awarded so many decorations to men who captured German machine-gun positions. The technique Brannen

learned from 1st Lieutenant Kilduff, called "marching fire," was an evolutionary method introduced to enable riflemen to cross no-man's-land against machine guns. It would not prove particularly effective.

11. Pvt. Carl Musgrove, USMC, enlisted June 9, 1917, and was wounded in action on June 10, 1918, at Belleau Wood. He had rejoined the 80th Company in July. U.S. Marine Corps, *Casualty List, AEF,* USMC.

12. Maj. Ernest C. "Bull" Williams, USMC. 1st Lieutenant Sellers of the 78th Company described him as "a simple kind of soul who liked to leave everything up to the adjutant while he would try to get up to the front line with an automatic rifle." Gunnery Sergeant Paradis called him "Bolo" Williams and was convinced that the major was both a drunk and the source of most of the avoidable miseries suffered by the battalion. 2nd Lt. Graves B. Erskine, who later commanded a marine division on Iwo Jima, thought that Major Williams "was not the best map reader in the world" and "didn't listen to his junior officers very much." As a lieutenant in the Dominican Republic in 1916, Williams audaciously had led twelve marines against three hundred guerrillas barricaded in a *fortaleza* (fort). Williams captured the small fort and a hundred of the guerrillas and received the Congressional Medal of Honor for his courage. Lt. Col. James McBrayer Sellers, "The 78th Company at Blanc Mont," *Marine Corps Gazette* 77, no. 11 (Nov. 1993): 45; Paradis, "Memoirs of Don V. Paradis," 174; and Erskine, "Interview," 62. For Williams' service in Haiti, see Ivan Musicant, *The Banana Wars* (New York: Macmillan, 1990), 270.

13. Brannen undoubtedly is referring to Capt. Wethered Woodworth, USMC, an extra captain (not the commanding officer) in the 79th Company. Woodworth had been wounded at Soissons and joined the 79th Company on Sept. 7, 1918. He was evacuated for wounds again on Sept. 15. U.S. Marine Corps, *Casualty List, AEF,* USMC. It appears from Brannen's memoir that Woodworth took command of the 80th Company when Captain Coffenberg was wounded.

14. Pvt. Florian L. Frillman, USMC, enlisted on May 29, 1917. Gunnery Sgt. Paradis recommended "Scatterbrain" for the Silver Star he received for his actions at St. Mihiel. MacGillivray and Clark, *History of the 80th Company,* iv; and Paradis, "Memoirs of Don V. Paradis," 119.

15. Pvt. Roland W. Hine, USMC. U.S. Marine Corps, *Casualty List, AEF*, USMC.

16. MacGillivray and Clark, *History of the 80th Company*, ii, records seventeen marines killed at St. Mihiel. Most of these casualties resulted from the action on Sept. 15. Spaulding and Wright, *Second Division AEF in France*, 48, lists fifty-nine killed in action and nine dead of wounds—the 80th Company suffered ¼ of all the fatal casualties in the entire 6th Marine Regiment for the St. Mihiel operation. For the 80th Company, St. Mihiel had been no walkover.

17. Helen Huntington Astor, first wife of New York industrialist, socialite, and philanthropist Vincent Astor. Linda Gillies, director, Vincent Astor Foundation, to the annotator, Owen.

Chapter 5: Blanc Mont

1. Smythe, *Pershing*, 174–75.

2. Maj. Gen. John A. Lejeune, *The Reminiscences of a Marine* (Philadelphia: Dorrance and Co., 1930), 342.

3. Ernst Otto, *The Battle at Blanc Mont*, trans. Martin Lichtenburg (Annapolis, Md.: U.S. Naval Institute, 1930), 15. Otto, a German officer who served at Blanc Mont, wrote this history of the campaign from the German perspective.

4. *History of the Sixth Regiment*, 32.

5. Maj. Edwin D. McClellan, "The Battle at Blanc Mont Ridge," pt. 2, *Marine Corps Gazette* 7, no. 2 (June 1922): 206–11.

6. *History of the Sixth Regiment*, 33–34.

7. "Scatterbrain" received a gunshot wound to the left arm on Oct. 4, the day after Brannen was evacuated. Frillman was evacuated to the U.S. on Dec. 22 for a subsequent discharge. U.S. Marine Corps, *Casualty List, AEF*, USMC.

8. Pvt. Lee N. Sherwood, USMC, was awarded the Silver Star and French Croix de Guerre for his actions at Blanc Mont. MacGillivray and Clark, *History of the 80th Company*, iv.

9. The 2nd Division artillery had been reinforced at Blanc Mont by the guns of the French 61st Division. 2nd Division Field Order No. 35, dated Oct. 2, 1918, in McClelland, "Battle at Blanc Mont Ridge," pt. 2, *Marine Corps Gazette* 7, no. 2 (June 1922): 207.

10. This was undoubtedly the regimental aid station of the 6th Marines, set up in a captured German subterranean hospital late on the afternoon of Oct. 3. It lay on the Sommepy–St. Etienne

road; the battalion aid stations had all set up on the crest of Blanc Mont. The regimental surgeons treated casualties passed back from the battalion aid stations here, or sent the more severely wounded back to a field hospital at Sommepy by litter bearer or ambulance. Strott, *Medical Department of the U.S. Navy,* 104–105.

The "major" was no doubt a lieutenant commander of the Navy Medical Detachment. The Marine Corps never has had its own surgeons, hospital corpsmen, or chaplains; the navy provides these specialists. In WWI, marines addressed naval officers serving in the 4th Brigade by the equivalent marine rank.

The surgeon who tagged Brannen for evacuation may well have been Lt. Comdr. Joel T. Boone, MC, USN, a highly decorated surgeon who was awarded the Distinguished Service Cross for his service at Belleau Wood and the Congressional Medal of Honor for his actions during the medical breakdown at Soissons. Boone is the only lieutenant commander who can be pinpointed at the 6th Marines Aid Station on Oct. 3. He later served as presidential surgeon to Warren Harding, Calvin Coolidge, and Herbert Hoover. He retired from the navy as vice admiral after World War II and served as chief medical director of the Veterans Administration. Spaulding and Wright, *Second Division AEF in France,* 317. U.S. Army, *Records of the 2nd Division,* vol. 5, 6th Marines Regimental Surgeon Field Message, dated Oct. 3. File on Joel T. Boone, Congressional Medal of Honor Society.

11. The 80th Company lost fifteen men killed or died of wounds on Blanc Mont and many more wounded. MacGillivray and Clark, *History of the 80th Company,* 317. Many of these were hit by German machine guns in the Essen Hook, which the French had failed to overcome. At 1:55 P.M. on Oct. 4, "Bull" Williams noted that the 80th Company had been reduced to sixty marines, down from two hundred who had begun the attack the morning before. When the Marine brigade trudged off Blanc Mont on the Oct. 9, there were fewer still. *History of the Sixth Regiment,* 37.

Chapter 6: The Meuse-Argonne

1. Smythe, *Pershing,* 190–94, 202, 212.

2. Spaulding and Wright, *Second Division AEF in France,* 197–99.

3. Ibid., 201–205.

4. *History of the Sixth Regiment,* 45–48.

5. Spaulding and Wright, *Second Division AEF in France,* 199–200.

6. Maj. L. W. T. Waller, "Machine Guns of the Fourth Brigade," *Marine Corps Gazette* 4, no. 3 (Mar. 1920): 27.

7. Spaulding and Wright, *Second Division AEF in France,* 199–200.

8. Capt. Kirt Green was killed in action on Nov. 1, 1918, while issuing instructions to his platoon commanders. A German field gun the company was preparing to envelop killed or wounded all the company's officers in one shot. Paradis, "Memoirs of Don V. Paradis," 161.

9. Although counter-battery shelling had caused almost one hundred casualties in the 1st Battalion as it went over the top, the attack proceeded extraordinarily well. Spaulding and Wright, in *Second Division AEF in France,* the official 2nd Division history, remark that the marines "kept so well to schedule that there is a noticeable lack of detail in the American reports" (204–205). One of the German divisions took such a pummeling that it mustered only thirty-five officers and 242 men out of 2,400 infantrymen present before the attack. At 3:15 P.M., "Bull" Williams sent a messenger to Lee that the 2nd Battalion was sitting atop Barricourt Heights. *History of the Sixth Regiment,* 47.

10. By the morning of Nov. 3, the doughboys of the 3rd Brigade had passed through the marines and taken over the front. A heavy rain began, continuing almost without ceasing for over a week. As temperatures hovered just above freezing, the lightly-clad marines suffered horribly.

11. The 2nd Division reached the Meuse River on Nov. 7. As patrols began a reconnaissance for suitable crossing points, the Germans sent intermediaries through the Allied lines to seek an armistice. Throughout the armistice negotiations, Allied commanders were determined to maintain relentless pressure. Planning for the difficult river crossing continued.

Colonel Lee, the 6th Marines commander, tasked Brannen's 2nd Battalion to support the division's main crossing at Mouzon. The 5th Marines, in conjunction with a battalion of the 89th Division, would attempt a second crossing about a mile upstream, near Letanne. German artillery and machine guns could easily rake either crossing point from formidable high ground on the east bank.

The marines trudged toward their attack positions on the night of Nov. 10. Harassing artillery fire delayed the start. Engineers struggled to construct rickety pontoon bridges in the dark. Delay followed delay, as machine-gun and artillery fire disrupted every attempt to put a bridge across at Mouzon. As the chance to cross before daylight slipped away, the crossing was canceled "by mutual consent of the battalion commanders."

The 5th Marines managed to put parts of three battalions across before the armistice, at a cost of 435 casualties. For a detailed account of the Meuse River crossing, see Rolfe Hillman, "Crossing the Meuse," in *Marine Corps Gazette* 72, no. 11 (Nov. 1988): 68–73.

12. Brannen probably is referring to the 5th Marines crossing at Letanne, as his battalion did not cross the Meuse. But the possibility exists that Brannen swam across that night. In the late 1940s, while building a water gap in icy water up to his neck, Brannen remarked to his son J. P. that he "hadn't been that cold since the night he swam the Meuse." Private Brannen was an exceptional swimmer and may have joined a working party sent by the 6th Marines to help the engineers put the bridge across.

13. The 80th Company had lost nine marines killed in the Meuse-Argonne, but another two died of disease. Twenty-one were wounded, and sickness had dropped the company's fighting strength by another seventy-three. MacGillivray and Clark, *History of the 80th Company*, iii, 7. "Muster Roll of the 80th Company," Nov. 1918, in *Muster Roll of the U.S. Marines*, microfilm.

14. Sgt. Grover C. O'Kelley, USMC, was awarded the Distinguished Service Cross, the Navy Cross, and a Silver Star for his actions at Belleau Wood. MacGillivray and Clark, *History of the 80th Company*, iv.

Chapter 7: Army of Occupation

1. Strott, *Medical Dept. of the U.S. Navy*, 131–32.

2. Smythe, *Pershing*, 248–51.

3. Strott, *Medical Dept. of the U.S. Navy*, 141.

4. The superb M1918 Browning Automatic Rifle (BAR) weighed about 20 lbs. with a magazine of twenty rounds inserted, and was capable of automatic or semiautomatic fire. It remained the big punch of American rifle squads through the Korean War. A few marines had acquired BARs as early as October, when nimble

fingers unburdened quite a few greenhorns in the 36th Division of their BARs. Military police collected these from the marines on the road south of Sommepy. The 6th Marines received twenty-five BARs before going into the Argonne, but most automatic riflemen carried the obsolete Chauchat through the Armistice. *History of the Sixth Regiment,* 44; Strott, *Medical Dept. of the U.S. Navy,* 108; Sellers, "The 78th Company at Blanc Mont," in *Marine Corps Gazette 77,* no. 11 (Nov. 1993): 49.

5. Major Williams was relieved of his command on the march to Germany by Corps Comdr. Maj. Gen. John Hines, who evidently thought Williams did not run a very tight ship. J. M. Sellers, unpublished memoir, collection of William W. Sellers, 42–43. Williams was overseas again in the Dominican Republic in 1920. In 1921, while stationed at the Marine barracks in Quantico, Va., he was badly injured while breaking a horse and retired with disability. When Charles Lindbergh—a civilian, in peacetime—received the Medal of Honor for his solo flight across the Atlantic, Williams vowed in protest never to wear his medal again. He died of a cerebral embolism in Seneca Falls, N.Y., in 1940, having kept his vow. George Clark, correspondence with the annotator, Owen. Gordon Hardy, ed., *Above and Beyond: A History of the Medal of Honor from the Civil War to Vietnam* (Boston: Boston Publishing Co., 1985), 118.

Lt. Col. Clyde W. Metcalf, USMC, commanded the eastern region of marine forces in Nicaragua in 1929, and later ran the U.S. Marine Corps Historical Section. Musicant, *Banana Wars,* 349.

6. The officers of Brannen's battalion celebrated the occasion by urinating in the Rhine. Hillman, "Marines in the Rhineland Occupation," *Naval History* 3, no. 3 (Summer 1989): 12.

Chapter 8: General Pershing's Honor Guard

1. Maj. Frederick A. Barker, USMC, had led the 1st Battalion, 6th Marines, at St. Mihiel, Blanc Mont, and the Meuse-Argonne. Barker had commanded the marine detachment of the USS *Connecticut* ashore in Haiti in 1915 and was on hand when Smedley Butler took Fort Riviere from the *cacos.* Musicant, *Banana Wars,* 199–201. Awarded the Navy Cross for his service at Blanc Mont, he commanded the 2nd Battalion of the Third Army Composite Regiment, in which Brannen marched. Spaulding and Wright, *Second Division AEF in France,* 311.

2. The legend that Col. Harry Lee was related to Robert E. Lee was understandable and often repeated but completely groundless. Maj. Gen. Harry Lee, USMC, biographical file at the Reference Section, Marine Corps Historical Center, Navy Yard, Washington, D.C.

3. Brannen's suspicions of political maneuvering were not without merit. Pershing had some aspirations to become U.S. president and was disappointed when the Republican party nominated Warren Harding instead. Smythe, *Pershing,* 269–74.

4. Pvt. Roy A. Trow, USMC, died of wounds June 7, 1918. "Muster Roll of the 79th Company," June 1–30, 1918, in *Muster Roll of the U.S. Marine Corps,* microfilm.

5. Brig. Gen. Smedley Darlington "Blanco" Butler, USMC, also known as "Old Gimlet Eye," was the only marine officer ever twice awarded the Congressional Medal of Honor. As commanding general of the 5th Marine Brigade, Butler was severely disappointed to see no action in WWI. Butler instead was ordered to Camp Pontezan at the port of Brest. As a major embarkation port, the camp was a disaster; over a hundred men died of influenza the day he took command. Butler attacked the squalid camp with old-fashioned leatherneck leadership and discipline and soon greatly improved conditions. During the 1920s, he commanded all marines in China; upon his retirement, he ran the Philadelphia Police Department. Merrill L. Bartlett, *Lejeune: A Marine's Life, 1867–1942* (Colombia: University of South Carolina Press, 1991), 11–112, 159, 165–66.

When Brannen writes, "I was commanded by General Smedley Butler for a time," he undoubtedly is referring to the period when the Composite Regiment billeted in Brest before sailing home. Smedley Butler had been in Haiti until after Brannen joined the 80th Company. As camp commandant, Butler had authority over hundreds of thousands of soldiers and marines who passed through his camp en route to the front or back to the United States.

Afterword: Before the Footprints Fade

1. When Dad reentered service in 1942, he wore a ribbon with five stars. I assumed that there was a one-to-one correspondence between the stars and the clasps. That could be an error.

2. He had a short leave in August 1942. I went with him to visit his aging father. When we returned, Mother asked what they

had talked about. My answer was that they didn't talk about anything. They just grinned at each other.

3. Dad died at age seventy-eight of prostate cancer.

4. He was almost a vegetarian; he ate very little meat but drank lots of buttermilk.

5. He was accorded unusual respect by the locals. He wasn't the local squire or anything like that, but without question he was one of the most admired men about.

6. There hadn't been any stateside service for the hail dancer.

7. His son-in-law, who was larger than Dad and no slouch in the athletic arena, claims to have been unable to lift an end.

8. For many years, I have ventured into the deep snow. I've gone alone into the mountains on my snowshoes to camp at temperatures much below zero, but nothing is as cold as East Texas at near freezing.

9. My generation must have produced many hail dancers in Europe. There must have been an abundant supply of hail busters.

10. Once when he and I were fixing fence down near the creek bottom, the patches of sunlight through the trees caused him to mention that it reminded him of the sunlight falling on a German sniper's face at Belleau Wood.

11. It has been pointed out that my sentence is poor French. It is likely that the saleslady was not French.

12. The British did not return bodies to England, as did the U.S. They arranged for small cemeteries near where their people died. They have some three thousand cemeteries in France.

13. I was reminded of a monument to the dead of a B-24 crew which crashed on the slopes of First Halder near the Swiss village of Wurënlingen on Christmas Day, 1944. It is well cared for, and on certain days the children of the village place flowers there.

14. I once asked Dad where the machine gunner was, relative to his position. My memory is that he replied that the gunner was at his two o'clock, i.e., about 30 degrees off his front.

15. I have concluded that the best way to go World War I battlefielding is to get near the spot you want information about and then start walking on the crops.

16. John Toland, *No Man's Land* (Garden City, N.Y.: Doubleday, 1980), 342.

17. John W. Thomason, *Fix Bayonets!*, 45.

18. I once heard Dad express to his brother some contempt

for the rear-echelon troops in that, after his torn and bloody tunic was removed, one of them salvaged it, put it on, and strutted around. It may have been that Dad wanted to keep it as a souvenir.

19. It turned out that there was a bullet in his side. It was discovered in the X-rays taken during his terminal illness.

20. When I read of the 6th Regiment being designated as the primary assault unit for the Meuse crossing, I had a sense of dismay. I could not imagine his surviving being up front in another attack.

Bibliography

Unpublished Materials

Boone, V. Adm. Joel T. Biographical file. Congressional Medal of Honor Society, Patriot's Point, S.C.

Cates, Clifton B. Letters. Marine Corps Personal Paper Collection. Marine Corps Historical Center, Navy Yard, Washington, D.C.

————. "Personal Observations of the Taking of Bouresches." Marine Corps Personal Paper Collection. Marine Corps Historical Center, Navy Yard, Washington, D.C.

Clark, Paul H. Personal Papers. Madison Building, Library of Congress, Washington, D.C.

Denig, Robert. "Diary of a Marine Officer During the World War." Marine Corps Personal Paper Collection. Marine Corps Historical Center, Navy Yard, Washington, D.C.

Erskine, Maj. Gen. Graves B. Interview by Brig. Gen. Bemis M. Frank. Oral History Collection. History and Museums Division, Navy Yard, Washington, D.C.

Harbord, James G. Personal War Letters. Manuscripts Division, Library of Congress, Washington, D.C.

Lee, Maj. Gen. Harry. Biographical file. Research Division, Marine Corps Historical Center, Navy Yard, Washington, D.C.

Paradis, Don V. "Memoirs of Don V. Paradis, Former

Gunnery Sergeant, USMC." Transcript of an oral history conducted on September 17, 1973. Marine Corps Personal Paper Collection. Marine Corps Historical Center, Navy Yard, Washington, D.C.

Sellers, James McBrayer. Unpublished Memoir. Collection of William W. Sellers.

Starling, Capt. P. W. Extract from After-Action Report, 2nd Brigade, 1st Division, Aisne-Marne Campaign. Annotator's possession.

Thomas, Gerald C. Memoir. Marine Corps Personal Paper Collection. Marine Corps Historical Center, Navy Yard, Washington, D.C.

Vandoren, 1st Lt. Lucien H. "A Brief History of the Second Battalion, Sixth Regiment, U.S. Marine Corps," July 13–25, 1918. Clifton B. Cates Papers. Marine Corps Historical Center, Navy Yard, Washington D.C.

Published Materials

"Advance to the Rhine." *Marine Corps Gazette* 72, no. 11 (Nov. 1988): 74–77.

Asprey, Robert B. *At Belleau Wood*. New York: G. P. Putnam's Sons, 1965.

Bartlett, Merrill L. *Lejeune: A Marine's Life, 1867–1942*. Colombia: University of South Carolina Press, 1991.

Berry, Henry. *Make the Kaiser Dance*. New York: Arbor House, 1978.

Cates, Gen. C. B. *History of the 96th Co*. Washington, D.C.: U.S. Marine Corps, 1935.

Clark, George. *Retreat, Hell! We Just Got Here*. Pike, N.H.: Brass Hat, n.d.

Coffman, Edward M. *The War to End All Wars*. Madison: University of Wisconsin Press, 1986.

Cooperman, Stanley. *World War One and the American Novel*. Baltimore, Md.: Johns Hopkins University Press, 1967.

Cowling, Kemper F. *Dear Folks at Home—*. Boston: Houghton Mifflin Co., 1919.

Derby, Richard. *Wade In, Sanitary!* New York: G. P. Putnam's Sons, 1919.

Fenton, Charles A. "Ambulance Drivers in France and Italy, 1914–1918." *American Quarterly* 3 (1951): 326–43.

Gibbons, Floyd. *And They Thought We Wouldn't Fight*. New York: George H. Doran Co., 1918.

Harbord, James G. *The American Army in France, 1917–1918*. Boston: Little, Brown, 1936.

———. *Leaves from a War Diary*. New York: Dodd, Mead, 1925.

———. "A Month in Belleau Wood 1918." *Leatherneck* (June 1928): 10–12, 54.

Hardy, Gordon, ed. *Above and Beyond: A History of the Medal of Honor from the Civil War to Vietnam*. Boston: Boston Publishing Co., 1985.

Hillman, Col. Rolfe L. "Crossing the Meuse." *Marine Corps Gazette* 72, no. 11 (Nov. 1988): 68–73.

———. "Fighters and Writers." *Marine Corps Gazette* 72, no. 11 (Nov. 1988): 90–98.

———. "Marines in the Rhineland." *Naval History* 3, no. 3 (Summer 1989).

———. "Second to None: The Indianheads." *U.S. Naval Institute Proceedings* 103, no. 11 (Nov. 1987): 57–62.

History of the Sixth Machine Gun Battalion. Neufeld on the Rhine, Germany: 1919. Reprint, Pike, N.H.: Brass Hat, 1993.

History of the Sixth Regiment, United States Marines. Tientsin, China: Tientsin Press, 1929.

Horne, Alistar. *The Price of Glory*. New York: Penguin Books, 1981.

Jones, Lt. Gen. William K. *A Brief History of the 6th Marines*. Washington, D.C.: History and Museums Division, U.S. Marine Corps, 1987.

Lee, Maj. Burton. "How Lieut. Overton Went Over the Top." *Galveston* (Tex.) *Globe and Anchor,* Nov. 22, 1918. In John Overton, Biographical File, Reference Section, Marine Corps Historical Center.

Lejeune, Maj. Gen. John A. *The Reminiscences of a Marine*. Philadelphia: Dorrance and Co., 1930.

Lewis, E. R. "The 14-Inch Naval Railway Batteries in France." *Naval History* 5, no. 1 (Spring 1991): 41–45.

Liggett, Lt. Gen. Hunter. *A.E.F.: Ten Years Ago in France*. New York: Dodd, Mead, 1928.

Lofgren, Steven. "Unready for War: The Army in World War One." *Military History* (Spring 1992): 11–19.

McClellan, Major Edwin N. "The Aisne Marne Offensive." 2 pts. *Marine Corps Gazette* 6, no. 1 (Mar. 1921): 66–84; and *Marine Corps Gazette* 6, no. 2 (June 1921): 188–227.

———. "The Battle at Blanc Mont Ridge." 3 pts. *Marine Corps Gazette* 7, no. 1 (Mar. 1922): 1–21; *Marine Corps Gazette* 7, no. 2 (June 1922): 206–11; *Marine Corps Gazette* 7, no. 3 (Sept. 1922): 287–88.

———. "Capture of Hill 142, Battle of Belleau Wood, and Capture of Bouresches." 2 pts. *Marine Corps Gazette* 5, no. 3 (Sept. 1920): 277–313; *Marine Corps Gazette* 5, no. 4 (Dec. 1920): 371–405.

———. *The United States Marines in the World War.* Rev. ed. Washington, D.C.: Headquarters, U.S. Marine Corps, 1968.

MacGillivray, George C., and George Clark. *A History of the 80th Company, Sixth Marines.* Pike, N.H.: Brass Hat, n.d. Annotated unit history.

Marshall, S. L. A. *The American Heritage History of World War I.* New York: American Heritage Publishing Co., 1964.

Millett, Alan R. *The General: Robert L. Bullard and the Officership of the United States Army, 1881–1925.* Westport, Conn.: Greenwood Press, 1975.

———. *Semper Fidelis: The History of the United States Marine Corps.* New York: Macmillan, 1980.

Mooney, James L., ed. *Dictionary of American Naval Fighting Ships.* Rev. ed. Vol. 3. Washington, D.C.: U.S. Navy, 1977.

Moskin, J. Robert. *The U.S. Marine Corps Story.* New York: McGraw-Hill, 1982.

Musicant, Ivan. *The Banana Wars.* New York: Macmillan, 1990.

Nenninger, Timothy K. "American Military Effectiveness in the First World War." In *Military Effectiveness,* vol. 1: *The First World War.* Edited by Alan R. Millett et al. New York: Unwin Hyman, 1988.

Otto, Lt. Col. Ernst. "The Battles for the Possession of Belleau Woods, June 1918." *U.S. Naval Institute Proceedings* 54, no. 11 (Nov. 1928): 941–62.

———. *The Battle at Blanc Mont.* Translated by Martin Lichtenburg. Annapolis, Md.: U.S. Naval Institute, 1930.

Pershing, John J. *My Experiences in the World War.* 2 vols. New York: Frederick A. Stokes Co., 1931.

Pitt, Barrie. *1918: The Last Act.* New York: Ballantine Books, 1963.

Rockwell, Paul Ayers. *American Fighters in the Foreign Legion, 1914–1918.* Boston: Riverside Press, 1930.

Sellers, Lt. Col. James McBrayer. "The 78th Company at Blanc Mont." *Marine Corps Gazette* 77, no. 11 (Nov. 1993): 44–49.

Shulimson, Jack. "The First to Fight: Marine Corps Expansion, 1914–1918." *Prologue* (Spring 1976): 5–16. Reprinted in *Marine Corps Gazette* (Nov. 1988).

Simmons, Brig. Gen. Edwin H. "The First Day at Soissons." *Fortitudine* (Summer 1993).

———. "The Second Day at Soissons." *Fortitudine* (Fall 1993).

———. *The United States Marines: The First Two Hundred Years, 1775–1976.* New York: Viking Press, 1974.

Smith, W. H. B. *Small Arms of the World.* 10th ed. Revised by Joseph E. Smith. Harrisburg, Pa.: Stackpole Co., 1973.

Smythe, Donald. *Pershing: General of the Armies.* Bloomington: Indiana University Press, 1986.

Spaulding, Oliver L., and John W. Wright. *The Second Division American Expeditionary Force in France, 1917–1919.* New York: Hillman Press, 1937. Reprint, Nashville, Tenn.: Battery Press, 1989.

Stallings, Laurence. *The Doughboys: The Story of the AEF, 1917–1918.* New York: Harper and Row, 1963.

Strott, George C. *The Medical Department of the United States Navy with the Army and Marine Corps in France in World War I.* Washington, D.C.: U.S. Navy, 1947.

Thomason, Capt. John W., Jr. *Fix Bayonets!* Washington, D.C.: Marine Corps Association, 1925.

———. "The Marine Brigade." *U.S. Naval Institute Proceedings* 54, no. 11 (Nov. 1928): 941–62.

U.S. American Battlefield Monuments Commission. *American Armies and Battlefields in Europe.* Washington, D.C.: U.S. Government Printing Office, 1938. Reprinted for the U.S. Army, Center of Military History, 1992.

———. *2nd Division Summary of Operations.* Washington, D.C.: U.S. Government Printing Office, 1938.

U.S. Army. *Field Service Regulations, 1914, Corrected to April, 1917.* Washington, D.C.: War Department, 1917.

U.S. Army. *Instructions for the Offensive Combat of Small Units.* Adapted from the French edition. Headquarters, American Expeditionary Forces, France, 1918.

U.S. Army. *Manual for Commanders of Infantry Platoons.* Translated from the French. Washington, D.C.: Army War College, 1917.

U.S. Army. *Records of the 2nd Division (Regular).* 9 vols. Washington, D.C.: Army War College, 1927.

U.S. Army. *Translations of War Diaries of German Units Opposed to the 2nd Division (Regular), 1918.* 9 vols. Washington D.C.: Army War College, 1927.

U.S. Marine Corps. Marine Corps Historical Center. Research Section. *Casualty List, American Expeditionary Forces.*

———. *Muster Roll of the U.S. Marine Corps.*

U.S. Navy. *The United States Naval Railroad Batteries in France.* Washington, D.C.: Naval Historical Center.

Vandiver, Frank E. *Black Jack: The Life and Times of John J. Pershing.* College Station: Texas A&M University Press, 1977.

Visconage, 1st Lt. J. M. "The Art of Recruiting." *Marine Corps Gazette* 71, no. 11 (Nov. 1986): 35–48.

Waller, Maj. L. W. T., Jr. "Machine Guns of the Fourth Brigade." *Marine Corps Gazette* 4, no. 3 (Mar. 1920): 1–31.

"Watch on the Rhine." *Marine Corps Gazette* 72, no. 11 (Nov. 1988): 78–87.

Wiegley, Russell F. *The American Way of War: A History of U.S. Military Strategy and Policy.* New York: Macmillan, 1973.

Williams, Brig. Gen. R. H. "The Fourth Marine Brigade." 4 pts. *Marine Corps Gazette* 64, no. 4 (Nov. 1980): 58–68; *Marine Corps Gazette* 64, no. 5 (Dec. 1980): 59–64; *Marine Corps Gazette* 64, no. 6 (Jan. 1981): 63–68; *Marine Corps Gazette* 64, no. 7 (Feb. 1981): 56–60.

Index

143n. 12; and relief from command, 148n. 5; at St. Mihiel, 40, 42, 99–100

Williams, Pvt. Forest (Red), 31, 137n. 11

Wilson, Woodrow, 4, 37

Woodworth (Woodall), Capt. Wethered, 42, 143n. 13

World War I, 3–4, 107–108; and American strategy, 37–38; and artillery support tactics, 142n. 10; and combat training, 9–10; and Germany, 12–13, 44, **120**; railroads in, 52; and remnants in the land, 106–107; and tanks, 53, 90, 136n. 10

World War II, 81, 108

Xammes, France, 40, 99

Yale University, 22, 124n. 4